Gwendolen M. Carter

CONTINUITY AND CHANGE
IN SOUTHERN AFRICA

Co-Publishers:
African Studies Association
Center for African Studies
University of Florida

Copyright © 1985: Crossroads Press
Continuity and Change in Southern Africa
Includes bibliographic essay. Index.
Carter, Gwendolen M.

ISBN # 0-918456-57-6

SEP   1988

THE CARTER LECTURES ON AFRICA

The Center for African Studies is fortunate to have Professor Gwendolen M. Carter as a member of its faculty. Since January 1984, Professor Carter has stimulated research, study, and teaching by sharing with Florida faculty and students alike her unique insights and wealth of knowledge about contemporary Africa.

In recognition of Gwendolen M. Carter's outstanding scholarly contribution to the study of African politics, and in honor of her association with the University and the Center, the Center for African Studies at the University of Florida has established the Carter Lectures on Africa.

Each year two to three leading Africanist scholars will be invited to present the Carter Lectures. During two consecutive years, each lecturer will examine a broadly similar topic. After five or six lectures on the same topic have been presented, they will appear as an edited volume providing a unified and demonstrable contribution to a significant African issue.

It seems fitting that the present collection, based on Dr. Carter's inaugural lectures, stand as the first volume in what we believe will be a distinguished series of books on African affairs by prominent African scholars.

CONTENTS

FOREWORD

On July 20, 1985, President P.W. Botha declared a "state
of emergency" in South Africa. His declaration was
in response to more than a year of violence and unrest
that had cost the lives of over five hundred South
Africans, all but a few of whom were Africans. By
taking this step, President Botha was acknowledging
implicitly that the extensive measures of coercive
rule through which South Africa's white minority have
governed that country were no longer sufficient. The
African challenge to continued white rule--indeed some
may wish to say the African revolution--had reached
a point where the authorities believed they needed
even more drastic coercive measures if they were to
maintain their control.

South Africa's renewed efforts to stamp out dissent
within its borders and to impose its own particular
version of law and order have presented both its
neighbors and the United States with further problems.
The Reagan administration's policy toward South Africa
has been one of "constructive engagement," whereby
it has sought to utilize friendly persuasion to encourage
the South African government to institute reforms of

the apartheid system. The July 20th state of emergency declaration vividly revealed the bankruptcy of constructive engagement, a bankruptcy that Congress had already recognized with the passage of bills in both the House and the Senate calling for sanctions against South Africa. At the moment, the U.S. seems to lack a coherent policy toward South Africa, for the administration is lamely defending constructive engagement and is seeking to thwart congressional sanctions legislation through threatening a veto. The real problem the administration confronts, however, and the nation as well, is not sanctions legislation but constructing a viable South African policy.

South Africa's neighbors, that is the countries that make up the Southern African Development Coordination Conference (SADCC) bloc, also confront a further set of problems. The strengthening internal African challenge to South African governmental authority has led not only to more coercive measures but also to stepped up governmental efforts to eradicate external bases of support for the African revolt within South Africa. Raids into neighboring countries to destroy supposed African National Congress bases, such as the one in the Spring of 1985 aimed at Gaborone, Botswana, support for dissident elements that destabilize the other countries in the region, and so forth are likely to increase in the months ahead as the South African government struggles to retain control of the situation in the country. Turmoil within South Africa also poses an economic problem to the other states of the region. Dependent as they are on transportation, communications, manufactured goods, and services from South Africa, disruption of the South African economy will have serious repercussions throughout Southern Africa. SADCC thus must grapple with new issues as well as those which led to its formation in the first place.

The African challenge to coercive rule thus emerges not only as a crucial issue for South Africans but also for the United States, the SADCC countries, and the world as a whole. To understand why this challenge has reached its current level of intensity, what direction events are likely to take in the months and years ahead, how the United States and other countries should respond to the trend of events, and what the long-range implications are, one has to get behind the headlines, the television coverage, and the statements of politicians and diplomats. For this, there is no better starting point than the published books and articles of Gwendolen M. Carter.

Gwendolen Carter is a scholar with both a broad and a detailed knowledge of South Africa and its people. Her work in the area covers nearly four decades. Complementing her knowledge of South Africa is a thorough first-hand acquaintance with developments over the same period of time elsewhere on the continent. The present collection of Professor Carter's essays and speeches, Continuity and Change in Southern Africa, constitute her most recent contribution toward a better understanding of the events that have caused South Africa to become one of the year's top news stories.

This book originated from the two inaugural Carter Lectures on Africa, which Professor Carter presented at the University of Florida in the Fall of 1984. These lectures appear in their present form as Chapters Three and Four. The balance of the chapters consist of further recent writings and lectures of Professor Carter. The Center for African Studies at the University of Florida has established the Carter Lectures on Africa as a means of acknowledging our pleasure at having Professor Carter as a colleague and a senior advisor in the Center as well as honoring her for her distinguished career of African scholarship. It is therefore fitting that the present volume stand as

the first in what we believe will be a series of
distinguished books by leading scholars on Africa.

Dr. R. Hunt Davis, Jr., Director
Center for African Studies
University of Florida
Gainesville, Florida
August 1985

CHAPTER ONE
INTRODUCTION

Southern Africa at the foot of the vast African continent
has long been an area of notable international significance. Its strategic position on the historic route
from Europe to the Middle East and Asia, its gold,
chrome, manganese, and a host of other valuable minerals
have long attracted commerce and investments from Europe
and North America. The Portuguese, Dutch, and British
each left their mark on the area, but the most developed
and richest power inside Southern Africa in the 20th
century has been white-controlled South Africa. South
Africa has been independent since 1910, long before
its neighbors could respond to the drive for African
independence after World War II.

Since that time, however, growing self confidence
among Africans who control their own independent states,
and also among those within South Africa itself have
led to new alignments inside and outside that country
and throughout Southern Africa as a whole. These
developments have increasingly attracted international
attention, including that of the United States. The
three articles that form the core of this work thus

have an essential relationship although, naturally, each is concentrated on its own particular issues.

Chapter Two, "Coercive Rule in South Africa" describes the way in which the white minority in that country has long used the state's legislative and administrative powers to restrict the movements and opportunities of that country's peoples of color: the huge majority of indigenous Africans, the numerous Coloured (mixed blood), and the Indians, who were brought to South Africa in the late nineteenth century as indentured labor to undertake arduous tasks the Africans refused to do. Beyond these restrictions, however, the South African government has systematically developed a well articulated structure of controls on protests by word or deed.

Basic to South Africa's actions are its concern for its own security and that of the Afrikaner people. Thus it has developed a fearsome arsenal of punishments for those who act on behalf of organizations like the African National Congress (ANC) which had its genesis in 1912 and, although banned since 1960, has remained the standard bearer of protest against unjust laws and the promoter of changes to move South Africa toward a more just society. Fourteen years after the Treason Trial of ANC members ended in 1961 with acquittals for all the accused, the government instituted yet further trials in 1985 against office holders and allies of the multiracial United Democratic Front (UDF). Moreover, the African majority, already outraged at its exclusion from the new constitution, has been suffering from undisciplined police actions backed up by the army. As protests become more wide-spread and effective, so does the machinery of coercion.

Chapter Three, "United States Policies toward South Africa and Namibia," contrasts policies under Presidents Kennedy and Nixon in the sixties with those of President Carter and President Reagan's "constructive engagement."

While all have sought to ameliorate South Africa's apartheid policies, there have been major differences in the approaches of these different administrations. President Carter's administration was persistently critical of South Africa's internal repressions and actively sought Namibian independence. In contrast, American policies toward Southern Africa in the early days of President Nixon's administration and during those of President Reagan have been formulated largely within the context of a world wide competition between East and West rather than in terms of its members own particular needs. One result is that efforts to bring Namibia to independence have been handicapped by American insistence on relating it to the removal of Cuban troops from Angola.

The chapter on the Southern African Development Coordination Conference (SADCC) broadens the horizon to take in the nine majority ruled states that share Southern Africa with their apartheid neighbor. Their boundaries and development have been strongly marked by their colonial experience. SADCC's two Portuguese speaking states--Mozambique and Angola--have between them all the ports (except Tanzania's Dar-es-Salaam) through which seaborne commerce can be conducted with outside states. Of SADCC's seven English-speaking states, six are landlocked. Among them, Zambia and Tanzania are precariously linked by the Chinese-built Tazara railway; Botswana, Lesotho, and Swaziland are related fiscally as well as economically to South Africa through the Southern African Customs Union; and Malawi maintains as much separateness as possible. Zimbabwe, whose independence in 1980 was fostered by the so-called Front Line States--Botswana, Zambia, Tanzania, Angola and Mozambique--has linked itself with them in the multiple causes of developing more self-sufficience, and of bringing about the independence of Namibia.

The over-riding goal of SADCC's members is to work together to develop their own resources and to free themselves to the degree possible from dependence on South African facilities and production so as to reduce South Africa's influence throughout the region. Since all the SADCC states are still in early stages of development, they appeal for support for their projects to the mature states of Western Europe and to the United States and Canada, as well as to such international organizations as seem appropriate. Meeting annually with the donor community, SADCC gives account of its programs and plans as well as its needs.

While all SADCC's members have suffered from the prevailing drought, Zimbabwe's peasant farmers reaped an unusually good harvest in 1985. Mozambique, however, continues to suffer devastation caused by the Mozambique Resistance Movement, despite the March 1984 N'komati Agreement with South Africa.

Angola is still subject to South African raids which continue to stall progress toward the independence of Namibia. Moreover, a South African strike into Cabinda and an attack on Botswana in June 1985 threatened its relations with the United States as described in Chapter Three.

In the conclusion to Chapter Two, there is a brief reference to conditions within South Africa itself in the fall of 1984 when widespread rioting in the African townships, school boycotts, and an unprecedented two day stay-at-home by African unionized labor abundantly demonstrated the fury of the African majority at their exclusion from the expansion of representation in Parliament under the new Constitution and their harassment by the police. Rule in South Africa remains coercive, but those who suffer most from its restrictions no longer remain silent and inactive.

CHAPTER TWO
COERCIVE RULE IN SOUTH AFRICA

Our major task is to ensure that a white nation will prevail here. Every nation has the inalienable right to safeguard that which it has built for itself and for posterity. This then is our task...but we know that this cannot be done by suppressing those entrusted to our care; neither can they be denied the opportunity to develop fully. This is a lesson that history has taught us, and which we know only too well. It is disgraceful that the outside world associates the concept of Separate Development with oppression.

--Prime Minister H.F. Verwoerd
September 3, 1963[1]

I am surprised at the conditions that the government wants to impose on me. I am not a violent man. My colleagues and I wrote in 1952 to Malan asking for a round table conference to find a solution to the problems of our country, but that was ignored. When Strijdom was in power, we made the same offer. Again it was ignored. When Verwoerd was in power we asked for a national convention for all the people in South Africa to decide on their future. This, too, was in vain.
It was only then when all other forms of resistance were no longer open to us that we turned to armed struggle. Let Botha show that he is different to Malan, Strijdom and Verwoerd. Let him renounce violence. Let him say that he will dismantle apartheid. Let him unban the people's organization, the African National Congress. Let him free all who have been imprisoned, banished or exiled for their opposition to apartheid. Let him guarantee free political activity so that the people may decide who will govern them.
I cherish my own freedom dearly, but I care even more for your freedom.
Only free men can negotiate.
I cannot and will not give any undertaking at a time when I and you, the people, are not free.
Your freedom and mine cannot be separated. I will return.

--Nelson Mandela
February 10, 1985[2]

South Africa's white minority has long operated a smoothly running parliamentary system whose members are selected in regularly held elections, and whose processes follow accepted procedures. The country's courts are constantly in session and technically they are color blind. Examination of many of the laws they administer, however, reveals that they underwrite the discriminatory racial system commonly known as apartheid. They provide white administrators with broad grants of power to determine where members of other racial groups may live and under what circumstances they may legally enter white areas, sell their labor, or take up domicile. Enforcing these, and many other restrictions, particularly on the African majority, is a host of penal provisions at the disposal of the police, backed up, if necessary, by the army.

Control over the allocation of space, and provisions to ensure a steady supply of cheap labor have long been crucial to the well being and prosperity of the white minority. Early in the 19th century, white settler and colonial governments developed a variety of native policies, including African reserves, to aid their economic and political control of the indigenous population. After Union in 1910, efforts to evolve a uniform African policy were complicated, however, by the sharp division between the mine owners and the farmers over what its character should be. The former wanted subsistence agriculture in the African reserves to supplement the low wages they paid in the mines, while the latter wanted as much land and African labor for themselves as possible.

The Natives Land Act of 1913 designated certain areas as African reserves but prohibited Africans from buying, or independently occupying land outside of the seven percent of the country's area that was allocated to them, most of it in Natal and the Eastern Cape. Thousands of relatively prosperous African share croppers and cash tenants, as well as squatters, were pushed off the land and became semi-proletarianized.

Barely enough land was left to Africans to provide a subsistence base for migrant mine workers. Although promised more land in the Hertzog-Smuts "settlement" of 1936, the total land possessed by Africans today is still less than the 13.7 percent envisaged then. Moreover, through the 1936 arrangement, male Cape Africans lost their historic right to vote on the common roll for candidates for Parliament, a right which only they among the Africans possessed.

The Afrikaner Nationalist electoral victory in 1948 led to new and far reaching means to implement their cherished policies of racial separation. By that time, the impact of World War II had caused major population changes both on the farms and in the urban areas. In the latter, the 1951 census disclosed that Africans slightly outnumbered whites: 2.3 million to 2.1 million. Also undercutting their continued presence was the rapidly changing character of industrial development in South Africa, which was reflected also to a degree in agriculture and mining, from their heavy dependence on relatively unskilled labor to an increasing demand for skilled labor.

The response to the postwar situation by the new government was swift and drastic. Influx control regulations were rigidly enforced against both African men and women. These restrictions were based mainly on older legislation, in particular the Natives (Urban Areas) Act of 1923, which turned all towns into "proclaimed areas" in which no African could remain legally for more than 72 hours unless he or she had labor bureau approval as migrant labor, or met so-called Section 10 provisions. These qualifications were and are: birth in the area; or 15 years of lawful residence; or service with the same employer for ten continuous years; or being the wife, son, or unmarried daughter of someone fulfilling those conditions. Coupled with the requirement that all male Africans (and subsequently also African women) carry a pass, the hated badge of servitude, these provisions led to massive endorsing out of large numbers of previously urban African residents--456,000 from twenty-three towns between 1956 and 1963.

In addition, The Resettlement of Natives Act, 1954, was used to force some 60,000 Africans from the so-called Western Areas to a new section farther outside Johannesburg. African freehold rights in certain urban areas also came under attack and, in a process that only recently ended, were abolished in three suburbs of Pretoria which were turned over to white occupancy and ownership.

It has not only been Africans who have suffered resettlement since the Nationalist government took office. The Group Areas Act of 1950 zoned all resi-dential areas for exclusive occupancy, or ownership by particular racial groups: white, Coloured, Indian, or African. Both the Coloured, who today form the majority population in the Western Cape, and the Indians, whose numbers are more or less equivalent to those of the whites in and around Durban, have suffered severely through rezoning.

Mass removals and population relocation remain constant features of contemporary South Africa. Their dimensions during the period from 1960 to 1982 have been meticulously documented through a large scale voluntary research effort known as "The Surplus Peoples Project." Started in 1980, its results have been published, beginning in January 1983, in five volumes under the title of Forced Removals in South Africa. The details provided by these volumes reveal that over 3.5 million people (3,522,900 to be exact) have been removed, often by force, and resettled during the period. Three-quarters to four-fifths of these people have been Africans, and the rest, Coloured or Indians. The Project estimates that two million more members of these three groups were threatened with removal in the near future.

The Coloured, whose primary right to jobs in the Western Cape was long protected by the "Coloured preference" policy, suffered the loss of their historic District Six whose proximity to Cape Town's business section ultimately sealed its fate. While the Coloured with adequate resources can find private housing in the new city built at Mitchell Plains on the far side of Cape Town, the poor in that community must share with Africans the wind swept Cape Flats which are far from the kind of jobs they can hope to secure. Unprecedented rioting by the Coloured in 1976 and again in 1980 reflected their frustration.

Residential segregation of Indians in Durban is just as unpopular. Although the development of three new living areas on the edges of town--Chatsworth, Phoenix, and Newlands West--has reduced, if not eliminated, removals under the Group Areas Act, middle class Indians resent the white domination in housing in the central part of the city as well as in the government of Natal. Even the housing strategies for low income Indians extending over a twenty year period have only led, according to a recent analysis, to "impoverishment and resentment."

The major impact of forced resettlement has fallen, as can be expected, on the Africans. It is intimately correlated with the evolution of the "homeland", or Bantustan, or national states policy, the ultimate expression and essential feature of separate development. In 1959, the Promotion of Bantu Self-Government Act recognized eight "Black national units" formed out of scattered reserves. Each had a distinctive ethnic character. Eight years before, the 1951 Bantu Authorities Act had replaced the local government administrative system in the reserves with what were considered more appropriate tribal, regional, and territorial authorities. Chiefs were given greater powers, the former elective aspects of administration were reduced, and overall ultimate white control was ensured.

In the same period, Africans were effectively cut off from their previous links to the country's law making system. The national Natives Representative Council, established in 1936 as an organ of consultation with the government, was abolished in 1951. Nineteen fifty-nine saw the abolition of the indirect representation of Africans in Parliament through specially chosen whites, which had been intended as a substitute for the 1936 loss by Cape Africans of their franchise on the common roll. The same process, despite much greater opposition by liberal whites, was used to remove the Coloured from the common voting roll in 1956, and their indirect representation by whites in 1968.

The African homelands, presently numbering ten, most of them situated on the periphery of South Africa, and several seriously fragmented, are in the goverment's view the appropriate representative entities responsible for the African majority. Those Africans domiciled in, or ethnically linked to the four homelands--Transkei, Bophuthatswana, Venda, and Ciskei--that have accepted the independence that no other state recognizes, were considered by the government to have lost their South African citizenship, although this much disliked provision has been modified recently. A fifth homeland, Kwa-Ndebele, is expected to accept independence soon. Its proximity to Pretoria makes possible daily commuting by fast trains to jobs in the city, considered by the government to be a particularly desirable way of securing labor without increasing the number of urban Africans.

From the early 1960's, the government's program of enforced resettlement of Africans in the homelands has been pushed ahead, sometimes by persuasion, often by coercion. It has had its impact from one end of the country to the other. Africans have been forced

out of towns, cities, and farming areas. While the
majority have been unskilled or semi-skilled, the dispos-
sessed have also included the skilled whose specialties
are no longer needed. The magnitude of what has gone
on is reflected in the fact that the proportion of
the total African population living in the homelands
had risen from 39.5 percent in 1960 to 54 percent in
1980. The flow continues.

High on the list of those being forced to leave
their homes are African communities that inhabit what
are commonly known as "black spots," that is settlements
that are surrounded by white owned or white occupied
land. Many of these African communities have long
histories. One of the few whose fate received the
publicity that has been generally lacking elsewhere
was Driefontein in the Transvaal. Exceptionally,
Driefontein had been established one year prior to
the Natives Land Act of 1913, having been bought the
year before on behalf of the Native Farmers' Association
of Africa, Ltd. by Pixley ka Isaka Seme, a founder
of the African National Congress, and its president
from 1930 to 1937. Driefontein was, therefore, on
freehold land. Its 5,000 inhabitants had productive
individual farming plots, wells, shops, schools,
churches, and sturdy houses. When numbers were painted
on them, a signal for resettlement, they joked about
it at first, but when they were painted on the grave-
stones, the people were outraged and protested. When
the police came on April 2, 1983, to accelerate their
move, Saul Mkhize, a migrant worker during the week,
who had written to Prime Minister Botha to appeal against
the move, argued with them. Impatient, the young white
policeman in charge returned to his car, took out his
gun, and shot and killed Mkhize. As the word spread,
many came to his funeral to protest, as much as to
mourn, but the removal was not stopped.

Neither African nationalists nor like-minded whites, Coloured, and Indians have accepted the government's policy of African separateness although it is under-written by a·fearsome array of coercive legislation. In 1952-53, Africans staged a nation-wide passive resistance campaign against "unjust laws." In 1955, a multi-racial Congress of the People affirmed in The Freedom Charter that "South Africa belongs to all who live in it, black and white." The government response was the long drawn out Treason Trial of 156 African, Coloured, Indian, and white leaders of nationalist and protest movements. They were acquitted by 1961.

In the meantime, however, a peaceful demonstration against the pass laws had led to the shooting of unarmed Africans at Sharpeville on March 21, 1960, killing sixty-seven and wounding more than 186 others. The national and international reactions to the massacre led to the proclamation of a state of emergency, the passage of the Unlawful Organizations Act, and its use to ban both the African National Congress, whose multiracial membership had long been in the forefront of the struggle for African rights, and its offshoot, the Pan-Africanist Congress.

White South Africans are privileged persons in com-parison to those in other racial categories, but they, too, may be subject to surveillance and harsh penalties for participation in protest movements which the government labels subversive, or for propagating their doctrines. The interpretation of such purposes is a matter of executive discretion through the almost unlimited grants of power under the Suppression of Communism Act, 1950, the Internal Security Act, 1970, and subsequent legislation. The 1950 Act not only dissolved the Communist Party but also empowered the State President to declare any other organization unlawful by simple proclamation without either giving it notice or the opportunity to testify in its own defense. These provisions were reaffirmed in the Unlawful Organizations Act of 1960.

Once an organization has been declared unlawful, there can be far reaching penalties for anyone shown to be or believed to be a member. One of the penalties is banning, which commonly involves restricting the person to a particular district, and to being with only one other person at a time. It may also require the person to report regularly, sometimes daily, to the local police station. An extreme form of banning can restrict a person to house arrest which means being forced to remain alone at home continuously except for designated periods for employment and for reporting to the police. The first person to suffer this extreme restriction was Helen Joseph, a white woman, who had been among the 156 persons in the Treason Trial. She had also been one of the leaders on August 9, 1956 of the massive multi-racial, though unsuccessful, protest held before the Union Buildings in Pretoria by twenty thousand women from all over the country against forcing African women to carry passes.

Detention without trial is another feature of South African security legislation. In 1963, the General Laws Amendment Act authorized the interrogation of persons held in solitary confinement for up to 90 days. Two years later, detention for 180 days to answer questions put by the authorities was made a permanent part of criminal procedure. In 1967, the Terrorism Act provided for indefinite detention without trial.

While there are major difficulties in determining who is being detained and where, the Detainees' Parents' Support Committee (DPSA), an informal association of parents and relatives of detainees, has collected a great deal of evidence to support its allegations that, since 1963, fifty-two persons have died in detention, and that in 1982, 191 persons were being held in detention without access to legal advice or to the courts.   If the homelands are taken into account, the number of detainees was 800 in 1981, 300 in 1982, and 127 in the first half of 1983.   The deaths in detention of the founder of the Black Consciousness Movement, Steve Biko, on September 12, 1977, and on February 5, 1982, of Neil Aggett, a white physician who worked with a black trade union, and on whose death there was a lengthy public inquest, are among the very few on which detailed information has been secured of what goes on in what the DPSA describes as "a virtually impenetrable system."

On June 30, 1983, the banning orders for the sixty-five persons then under that restriction lapsed in terms of Section 73 (12) of the revised Internal Security Act of a year before, but banning was immediately reimposed on ten of them.   The latter included Winnie Mandela, a prominent nationalist figure in her own right, and the wife of the leader of the African National Congress, Nelson Mandela, who has long been imprisoned for life.   Mrs. Mandela has also suffered banishment to Brandfort, a small town in the Orange Free State.   Another prominent person, Dr. Beyers Naude, a distinguished Afrikaans clergyman who has long maintained his stand against apartheid restrictions, was rebanned in October, 1982, but freed from all restraints in 1984.   He succeeded Bishop Desmond Tutu as Director of the South African Council of Churches after the latter was awarded the Nobel Prize and became Bishop of Johannesburg.

While there was a general sense of relief that banning restrictions were removed from many of those who had long suffered from them, the government's power to impose banning at will still remains intact.   It should be noted also that a new list drawn up by the Director of Security Legislation of those who cannot be quoted in South Africa either during their lifetime or thereafter includes 134 names and that, according to the Rabie Commission recommendations, more names can be added to it over the following four years.

Those persons subject to "listing" were originally the office bearers, members, or believed to be active supporters of groups declared by the government to be unlawful. Under Section 10 of the 1982 Internal Security Act, they now include persons of all races convicted after June of that year of government-defined communism, terrorism, or sedition. They were held by the court to include Ms. Barbara Hogan, whose membership in the African National Congress led to a ten year sentence of imprisonment for treason despite the fact that she was not charged with any overt act including demonstrations on its behalf. Section 10 also covers "printing, publishing or disseminating" any material in contravention of any government regulation, thereby enlarging the already very considerable anxieties and potential restrictions under which the South African press and other organizations must operate.

On November 3, 1983, white voters endorsed by a two-thirds majority a new constitution which established for the first time in the country's history a tripartite Parliament in which representatives of the 2,117,000 Coloured and of the 875,000 Indians each have their own chamber as the representatives of the 4,060,000 whites have long had. Each group is responsible for legislation affecting its own exclusive affairs as defined by the white President. National legislation, like the Group Areas Act, and the budget, however, is voted on jointly by the representatives in all three houses, among whom the white house commands a decisive majority. The new constitution also provided for a President, elected for five years by an electoral college in which whites also have a majority. Combining the powers of the former Prime Minister and of the State President, P.W. Botha, who is the President under the new constitution, became the most powerful individual in the country's history.

All three racial groups covered under the new constitution have been sharply divided in their reactions to it. The inclusion of Coloured and Indians in Parliament has been bitterly opposed by the right wing Afrikaner Nationalists led by Dr. Andries Treurnicht. The explicit exclusion of Africans, the country's majority population, from any role in the new constitution has led to sharp protests from every racial group. It also led to strikingly low participation by both Coloured and Indian registered voters for their candidates for Parliament, thirty percent of those eligible among the former and twenty percent of the latter. Since the percentage of registered voters in both groups had also been very low, the total number of eligible voters who voted was only 17.8 percent among Coloured and 14.1 percent among Indians.

For the 22 million Africans, their exclusion from the new constitution and the imposition on the townships of an unpopular third tier of local administration led to intense bitterness, unrest and sporadic violence--especially against those considered collaborators--as well as to country-wide school boycotts. Township bitterness and violence increased when the government sent in troops as well as police to attempt to establish order.

The character of the new constitution was also one of the factors leading to the formation of two new movements dedicated to fundamental change in South Africa. The largest of these movements--the United Democratic Front (UDF), organized formally on August 20-21, 1983--had been built up regionally from January on. A locally based front for some 400 affiliated groups including trade unions, churches and community organizations, it has an estimated membership of one to one and a half million people of all races. While the names of some of its patrons indicate a kinship with the banned African National Congress and The Freedom Charter's "South Africa belongs to all its people, black and white," the UDF has been careful to avoid any explicit relationship. Nonetheless, in February 1985 the government imprisoned sixteen of its leaders and charged them with treason. Their trial began officially in May, 1985. Some of the leaders of unaffiliated groups engaged in political confrontation are also on trial for treason, alongside UDF leaders.

Another grouping, the National Forum, launched June 11-12, 1983, specifies "racial capitalism" as a major target. Its most vocal adherents, The Azanian People's Organization, (AZAPO), demonstrated loudly against Senator Edward Kennedy during his visit to South Africa in January 1985.

The most promising development in South Africa has been the growth and stability of the African trade unions. Legalized in 1979, they have expanded into several confederations, of which the most prominent are the Federation of South African Trade Unions (FOSATU) with affiliates in the auto, steel and textile industries, and about 115,000 members, almost all African or Coloured, and the Council of Unions of South Africa (CUSA), a federation of nine all-African trade unions with about 148,000 members. Another union is the National Union of Mineworkers with some 90,000 members.

A planned two day stay-at-home protest in November 1984 in the Vaal Triangle townships by black trade unions demonstrated their anger at the African exclusion from the new constitution as well as at township administrators and inflated rents. It provided impressive evidence of discipline and had a strong impact.

The government owned SASOL (oil from coal) dismissed all its 6,000 African workers in retaliation for joining the strike but, finally, under persistent pressure from its own chemical union (CWIU) and the threat of a general strike, took nearly all of them back. Much the same process of exerting internal and external pressures ultimately restored the jobs of most of the miners dismissed in the spring of 1985 by Anglo-American in response to work slowdowns and threats.

In opening the first working session of the new tricameral Parliament in January, 1985, President Botha spoke in general of a future cooperative coexistence in South Africa in which "there is no domination of one population group over another" requiring "self determination for each group over its own affairs and joint responsibility for, and cooperation in, common interests," but without specifying how it would be done. He also suggested there might be extension of full property rights for Africans in certain urban areas in South Africa and the so-called "self-governing states," and restrictions on influx control.

Most surprising, was Botha's subsequent overture to Nelson Mandela, the long imprisoned acknowledged leader of the African National Congress whose activities were becoming increasingly noticeable. Botha offered to release Mandela from prison if he would "renounce violence." Mandela's reply appears in the preface to this chapter. Although the offer of release was subsequently withdrawn, there continue to be rumors of discussions through third parties seeking some modus vivendi between the government and its most significant adversary.

What had seemed a more encouraging attitude by the government was seriously clouded by the police killings during their January raid on the shantytown known as Crossroads outside Cape Town where some 50,000 to 100,000 Africans have been living precariously for the last decade. National and international reactions to the violence led to a joint arrangement that in return for providing job permits to Crossroad residents for approximately a year and a half, some 40,000 of its

100,000 members would agree to move to Khayelitsha, the new settlement that the government has established in the sand dunes nearer the ocean, but thus still farther from Cape Town and potential jobs. Already there are complaints by those who have moved that the houses provided are too small and difficult to expand and the travel costs are too high so the situation remains uncertain at best.

Still more shocking have been the brutal police actions against peaceful demonstrations, and worst of all against massive funeral processions, as at Uitenhage on the 25th anniversary of the Sharpeville massacre that had shocked the world at that earlier time. Testimony by members of the Black Sash and others indicate that the police, both white and black, have also been terrorizing townships in the eastern region of the Cape and perhaps elsewhere.

On July 20, 1985, the South African government declared a state of emergency in the thirty-six townships around Johannesburg and in the Eastern Cape where the strongest protests against police actions and demands for rights have been centered. It was the first time it had done so since the Sharpeville massacre. While the government already had vast powers at its disposal, the state of emergency added two significant features to their functioning. While these powers remain in effect, no act by the police or any other government agency in the specified areas can be used in the future as a basis for prosecutions, thereby providing unlimited opportunities for official violence. The state of emergency also made possible control over the coverage of events in the press. Initially, there appeared to be little curbing of what was reported either within South Africa or abroad but only after its termination can that be determined.

Even without the state of emergency, the South African government possesses and not infrequently uses its vast powers to try to shape its people's lives and livelihoods to fit the overall pattern of racial segregation and conformist behavior which is embodied in so many of its laws and regulations and implemented through their administration. Without habeas corpus, even under normal circumstances, South Africa can be accurately described as a police state.

South Africa's white military leaders have described the basic conflict within the country as eighty percent political and only twenty percent military. Its chief military commander said in 1983 that the government must "win the hearts and minds of our indigeneous people." So far, there is little, if any evidence that the new constitution, or any other government initiative or action has yet served to build an enhanced sense of unity within the country.

Only when responsible members of the government and industry are prepared to sit down with genuine representatives of the mass of the people to consider their demands for rights seriously, and to begin to implement the new patterns of life and activities for which they are striving, will South Africa begin to move toward a genuine degree of stability and relative harmony.

NOTES

1. Verwoerd's statement is quoted in "Crisis in World Conscience," Pretoria, Department of Information, 1964.

2. Nelson Mandela's response to President P.W. Botha's offer to release him from prison if he would foreswear violence. As reported in the Rand Daily Mail; Mandela's response was read by his daughter, Zinzi, to a mass rally in Soweto on February 10, 1985.

CHAPTER THREE
UNITED STATES POLICIES
TOWARD
SOUTH AFRICA AND NAMIBIA

The 1984 electoral campaign provided striking evidence that United States policies toward South Africa and Namibia were regarded by both Republicans and Democrats as significant features of their overall foreign policies. Both parties included clauses on those issues in their electoral platforms, and vigorously supported their own positions and criticized those of their opponents at their conventions and during the campaign. What captured the American imagination, however, and gave rise to country-wide demonstrations supporting a range of sanctions and progress toward anti-apartheid legislation in both the House of Representatives and the Senate, was the civil disobedience campaign led by the Free South Africa Movement (FSAM). This campaign has resulted in thousands of Americans courting arrest by demonstrating daily, Monday through Friday, in front of the South African Embassy in Washington D.C.

The genesis of the Movement was a sit-in at the South African Embassy on November 21, 1984, which led to the arrest and overnight imprisonment of three prominent black Americans: Congressman Walter Fauntroy,

U.S. Civil Rights Commissioner Mary Frances Berry, and TransAfrica Director, Randall Robinson. They were protesting the detention of thirteen black South Africans involved in planning the two day protest strike in November, 1984, by their black trade unions against the use of army personnel as well as police to harass demonstrators in the black townships near Johannesburg. The latter had been angered by the exclusion of Africans from the new South African constitution as well as local rent and other grievances.

The daily courting of arrests since that time has served to publicize the three major goals of the Free South Africa Movement: the release of all South African prisoners; the extension of political rights to all South Africans; and the dismantling of President Reagan's policy of "constructive engagement."

The Movement expanded quickly and by the end of April, 1985, there were Free South Africa chapters in twenty-three cities throughout the country. Activists have also attempted to stop the sale of Krugerrand and again captured headlines on May 5 when five members of its steering committee staged a sit-in at the Washington Office of Deak-Perera, one of the largest nationwide distributors of the South African gold coin.

An indication that the Movement's activities and the public's response have had an impact on the Reagan administration came in mid-March when the United States cast a rare vote against South Africa on a United Nations Security Council resolution condemning the killing of protestors at Cape Town's squatter camp, Crossroads. The resolution also condemned the treason charges brought against sixteen leaders of the United Democratic Front, the multiracial movement based on hundreds of local church and other groups and numbering over a million members. While vetoing a call by the six non-aligned members of the Security Council for mandatory sanctions against South Africa if it failed to eradicate apartheid,

both the United States and Britain abstained but allowed
to pass on June 26, 1985, a resolution condemning its
state of emergency and the arrest of thousands of
Africans. It was the strongest measure approved by
the Council against South Africa since the adoption
of the arms embargo in 1977.

No less active than the FSAM have been thousands
of students demonstrating in more than a hundred colleges
and universities throughout the country to urge their
institutions to divest their portfolios of stocks in
companies doing business in South Africa. Some protests
sought the much more far reaching process of disinvestment by corporations through closing their interests
in South Africa. Students and others also demanded
that banks cease making loans to South Africa, all
part of the general pattern of attempting to reduce,
if not terminate, American economic ties with South
Africa.

The American economic stake in South Africa is very
considerable. At the end of 1984, the value of direct
investments totalled over two billion dollars. Total
lending by American banks to South African interests
had reached $4.7 billion in 1984, twice the amount
in 1978. American ownership of South African mining
shares has been estimated at $6.5 billion.

Probably the most visible role of American companies
in South Africa is by their oil companies, since South
Africa has no domestic oil resources of its own. Mobil
was listed in mid-1985 as having the largest assets--$400
million--among United States investors in that country,
with Ford and General Motors listed as the next two.
Chevron, Exxon, Phillips, Texaco and Standard Oil of
Ohio also have service stations spread around South
Africa. Threatened by boycotts, that country places
great wieght on synthetic fuel developed from its own
coal. This requires complicated processing and refining.
An American company, Fluro, was managing contractor

during the 1970's for South Africa's $6 billion SASOL oil-from-coal facilities in the eastern Transvaal and presently has a maintenance contract for a South African nuclear facility.

Another highly important field in South Africa for American companies is computer manufacturing. IBM, Control Data Corporation, and Burroughs are the most prominent companies. It should be noted that the Canadian government in announcing on July 7, 1985, some of the broadest sanctions by a Western state against South Africa placed special restrictions on high technology sales of equipment such as computers to South African government agencies and state owned companies to prevent their use by police and other security forces.

In a major reversal of the Administration's opposition to economic sanctions against South Africa, President Reagan on September 9, 1985 instituted most of the trade and financial measures against apartheid which Congress could have imposed even over his veto. He banned the sale of computers to South African security agencies; barred most government loans; halted the import of Krugerrand; and stopped exports of nuclear technology until South Africa agrees to international accords preventing the spread of nuclear weapons. None of these measures will have a substantial effect on the economy of South Africa, or on American companies doing busienss there, still they were accompanied by a sharp condemnation of apartheid restrictions and a strong expression of concern over the increasing racial violence.

Anti-South African actions by states and cities can also have a considerable effect. Divestment laws have already been passed by the legislatures of Connecticut, Maryland, Massachusetts, Michigan and Nebraska, and a number of cities including Philadelphia, Washington, Boston, and New York have taken the same action.

In May 1985, Governor Cuomo announced that he would introduce legislation to require the gradual disinvestment of billions of dollars in New York State funds, including about $4.4 billion presently invested in employees' and teachers' pension funds. The divestment would begin in 1986 with companies doing business directly with the South African government or Namibia, and those others that have not signed the Sullivan code prescribing equal treatment for black and white workers. By 1990, it would affect all American companies in the state doing business in South Africa.

South African reactions to American divestment and divestiture actions have been varied. Some are enthusiastic but Kwa-Zulu's Chief Gatsha Buthelezi is strongly opposed on the ground that divestment would hurt black South Africans.

An indication of its national effect was provided by a statement presented to Senator Kennedy on his arrival in South Africa in January 1985 on behalf of six major employer bodies: Die Afrikaanse Handelsinstituut, The Association of Chambers of Commerce of South Africa, The Chamber of Mines of South Africa, The South African Federated Chamber of Industries, The National African Federation of Chamber of Commerce, and The Steel and Engineering Industries Federation--claiming to represent more than eighty percent of the employment strength of South Africa. In an explicit effort to stave off a ban on U.S. investments, trade restrictions, prohibitions on bank loans and procurement boycotts against American corporations doing business with South Africa, they pledged themselves to work for "a universal citizenship," "meaningful political participation for Blacks," "full participation for all South Africans regardless of race, colour, sex or creed," in the development of "a free and independent trade union movement," and "a private enterprise economy," as well as an end to "the forceful removal of people." Should they, indeed, live up to these pledges, they could have a major impact on the South African government.

While public attention has focused on the specific proposals for exerting influence on the South African government to make far reaching changes in its apartheid policies, American trade unions have quietly been developing their own direct relations with black South African trade unions in response to their requests. One example was that when the Ford Motor Company decided to shut down one of its plants near Port Elizabeth, thereby causing a serious loss of jobs that has aggravated the situation in that area, the United Auto Workers (UAW) met with Ford officials in Detroit to reinforce the concerns of the local black trade union that was meeting with its management in South Africa. The UAW, as well as other American unions, also have intervened on behalf of South African unions over problems in contract negotiations. Moreover, in its own contract negotiations with Chrysler in 1979, the auto workers won the right to veto South African related investments linked to their pension funds.

Two decades ago, the issues of Southern Africa seemed remote to most Americans, as well as to their government. The United States complied with the United Nations' sponsored arms embargo against South Africa in the early 1960's, and supported a variety of resolutions condemning apartheid. There was little, if any, general discussion on the issues, however, or positive use of American power, or even of its potential influence on situations in Southern Africa. There was a ritual opposition to colonialism and apartheid but little concern. Indeed, President Nixon's first term was marked by a strong bias toward Southern Africa's white regimes as providing the necessary basis of stability and "constructive change" in the region.

This negative attitude in the early days of the

Nixon administration toward promoting change in Southern
Africa, and particularly within its white regimes,
went so far as to lead it to partially lift the arms
embargo against South Africa, and to oppose rather
than support United Nations resolutions critical of
apartheid. Most strikingly, the Nixon administration
yielded to domestic pressure and acquiesced in the
1971 Byrd amendment that enabled the United States
to import Rhodesian chrome in violation of the United
Nations-mandated economic sanctions that were imposed
on Rhodesia following Ian Smith's illegal unilateral
declaration of independence on November 11, 1965.

The mid-1970's, however, provided the Nixon and
Ford administrations with alarming evidence of growing
instability in the white-controlled states of Southern
Africa. Of particular concern was the intrusion of
Soviet and Cuban arms and personnel into the civil
war in Angola. At the same time, the African nationalist
onslaught on the Ian Smith regime in Rhodesia was growing
in intensity. The Portuguese were yielding control
in Mozambique. Moreover, in 1976, South Africa's largest
peri-urban African township, Soweto, erupted in protest
at apartheid restrictions. The startling success of
the Arab oil boycott also raised overall concern
regarding the West's continued access to the rich mineral
resources of Southern Africa should they come under
the control of unfriendly Soviet-oriented states.

As events moved quickly in Angola, Secretary of
State Henry Kissinger sought to block Soviet and Cuban
support for the Marxist-oriented People's Movement
for the Liberation of Angola (MPLA). However, the
Tunney resolution in the Senate prevented him from
taking the overt military actions he desired. Subsequently, the Clark amendment in the House forbade direct
or indirect assistance to Angolan factions. South
African troops, invading Angola from the south with
tacit American approval, failed to change the situation

and were forced to withdraw. The MPLA was widely recognized as the legitimate government of Angola--although not yet by the United States--but remains forcefully opposed within the country by the Union for the Total Independence of Angola (UNITA).

During his remaining time as Secretary of State in the Nixon and Ford administrations, Kissinger sought to establish a containment policy governing the rest of Southern Africa, most notably in Rhodesia and Namibia. Engaging in shuttle diplomacy with the tacit support of the South African government, Kissinger succeeded in persuading the premier, Ian Smith, to accept a constitutional framework which would establish majority rule in Rhodesia within the next two years. These provisions proved unacceptable, however, to the Zimbabwe Patriotic Front, led at that time by Joshua Nkomo and Robert Mugabe, and also to their supporters, the Presidents of the Front Line States comprising Angola, Botswana, Mozambique, Tanzania, and Zambia.

Kissinger also sought, with little success, to persuade South African leaders to withdraw their forces from Namibia as demanded by Security Council Resolution 385. Despite South African protestations, Kissinger had little confidence in the constitution-making potential of the recently established Turnhalle Conference composed of representatives from the eleven ethnic divisions into which South Africa had divided the territory. Thus, although Kissinger had seized the initiative once more in United States-Southern Africa relations and prepared the way for new policies by the incoming Carter administration, there was no peace either in Rhodesia or in Namibia when Kissinger turned over the office to his Democratic successor in 1977.

The Carter administration had good reasons for adopting a more liberal and African-oriented policy toward Southern Africa than Kissinger had pursued.

President Carter's strong humanitarian feelings made apartheid repugnant. Moreover, his party's support by liberal academics, church groups, and black Americans had contributed substantially to its narrow victory at the polls. In addition, African countries, most notably Nigeria, which had replaced South Africa as the United States' largest African trading partner, commanded increasing international attention. Thus policies favoring African interests rather than reflecting fears of Soviet encroachment in Southern Africa seemed appropriate in the mid-1970's and also proved popular, at least in the early years of the Carter regime.

As the United States Ambassador to the United Nations, President Carter appointed Andrew Young, a distinguished black internationalist who had served as an effective congressman from Georgia (1973-1977). Young strongly supported United Nations policies in Southern Africa, and particularly in Rhodesia and Congress was quickly persuaded to repeal the Byrd amendment, thereby registering the new American commitment to aid in bringing Rhodesia to an acceptable independence.

In his 1980 article in Foreign Affairs,[1] Andrew Young maintains that the repeal of the Byrd amendment "helped create" a new atmosphere of "considerable trust" with both the British and the Africans. Thereafter, there was what he called a "free-flowing exchange of information" between the United States and Great Britain on the one hand, and with the Zimbabwe Patriotic Front, the Front Line States, and Nigeria on the other. African-Western talks over the next three years led to the Lancaster House negotiations out of which came Zimbabwean independence.

Throughout these and other negotiations, the Carter administration's respect for the Front Line States led it to support their initiatives rather than to continued attempts to force them to follow American leads. Behind this new posture was the belief that regardless of their particular ideology, the policies of independent African states would not threaten American interests unless the East-West conflict was brought specifically into the situation as it had been over Angola.

In its role in the Rhodesia-Zimbabwe negotiations, as well as in other African situations, the Carter administration studiously avoided the friendly posture toward South Africa that had marked the preceeding Ford-Kissinger period. The most dramatic example of its distinctive posture toward South Africa came during a joint South African-American meeting in Vienna, on May 19-20, 1977, when Vice-President Walter Mondale told Prime Minister Vorster that the American goal was full political participation by all South Africans. While it was after the meeting that Mondale affirmed that his words meant "one man, one vote," there had never been any doubt about his basic meaning, nor of Vorster's strong reaction against it, or of its impact on African thinking both inside and outside South Africa.

Despite its obvious distaste for South African policies, the Carter administration was slow to take any punitive action against that country. Several possible measures, like discouraging new investment and bank loans, were considered, but even the milder move of denying tax credits to investors was not adopted. Carter and Young appear to have shared a belief, for which they had very little evidence, that economic interactions between this country and South Africa could have a beneficial effect on race relations within the latter. Fortunately, in March 1977 the Reverend Leon Sullivan announced that twelve American companies had adopted a code of fair employment and non-segregation practices in South Africa which could be applauded.

In October 1977, however, a crackdown by the South African government on black consciousness organizations, the Christian Institute, and the major newspaper edited by an African, The World, followed the security police killing of Steve Biko, the outstanding South African black consciousness leader. These actions led the United States to join with its Western allies in support of a Security Council decision on November 4, 1977, that mandated an embargo on South Africa's acquisition of arms and related materials. Although a voluntary embargo already existed, the decision was psychologically significant since there had never before been a mandatory embargo against a United Nations member.

The second major Southern African issue with which the Carter administration was concerned was the future of Namibia. Taken from Germany during World War I and officially declared a mandate under the League of Nations, Namibia had been treated thereafter as virtually a fifth South African province. Moreover, after World War II, South Africa was the only country to refuse either to grant independence to a captured territory or to place it under the more rigorous United Nations trusteeship system. On the contrary, South Africa increasingly extended its own discriminatory legislation to Namibia, treating it as if it were part of its own territory.

Judicial redress was sought before the World Court in a long, drawn-out case which ended in 1966 without a decision. The General Assembly, with the United States voting in the affirmative, then revoked South Africa's mandate through Resolution 2145 on the ground of maladministration and resolved to take over the administration of Namibia itself until the territory reached independence. Subsequently, the International Court of Justice in an advisory opinion issued on June 21, 1971, reinforced the Assembly's action by declaring that since South Africa's presence in Namibia was illegal, it was under an obligation to "withdraw its administration immediately" and thus end "its occupation of the territory."

South Africa, however, refused to yield and began a long-range program of reorganizing the administration of the territory into white and ethnic African divisions. Representatives from these entities were then formed into the so-called Turnhalle Conference, as already noted, which on August 18, 1976, produced a short statement of principles suggesting "independence" by the end of 1978. The South West African Peoples' Organization (SWAPO), the exiled nationalist movement headed by Sam Nujoma, was never included in these discussions despite the fact that it is recognized as the authentic representative of the Namibian people by both the Organization of African Unity and the United Nations itself.

Confronting this situation, the Carter administration took the lead in organizing the so-called Contact Group composed of representatives of the five Western Security Council members--the United States, Great Britain, Canada, France, and West Germany--working closely with the Nigerians and with representatives from the Front Line States. Chaired by the American representative, Donald McHenry, the Contact Group undertook personal negotiations early in 1977, meeting in Pretoria with Prime Minister Vorster and other high-level South African figures. Subsequently, they conducted their own investigations in Namibia itself. Both in South Africa and in Namibia, the Contact Group made it clear that a Turnhalle "constitution" would in no sense be acceptable.

Following a seemingly endless series of meetings among all parties concerned with Namibia, Prime Minister Vorster agreed on April 25, 1978, to a United Nations sponsored transfer of power in Namibia. The Americans and the British pressured SWAPO to agree as well. A plan for a United Nations civilian and military operation in Namibia, paving the way for elections leading to Namibian independence, was unanimously approved by the Security Council on September 29, 1978, and embodied in Resolution 435. It was sponsored by the five members of the Contact Group, including the United States, and by Gabon, Mauritius, and Nigeria.

By that time, however, Prime Minister Vorster was already objecting to the size of the United Nations force that the Secretary-General suggested would be necessary to prepare for electing the government of an independent Namibia. In the light of subsequent developments, none of which have yet brought Namibia close to independence, it is worth noting that the Cubans in Angola were never mentioned during any of these exchanges.

The Carter administration was sensitive to the harsh conditions, as well as to the restiveness of the massive African majority in South Africa. It also recognized the growing importance of Nigeria with its huge oil reserves (making it second only to Saudi Arabia for American imports) and its determination to play a role in international affairs affecting Africa. Since that time, neither factor has played so important a role in determining the South African and Namibian policies of the United States but their impact has not been forgotten.

With the electoral victory of Ronald Reagan in November 1980, American policies toward Southern Africa changed substantially. The Carter administration had at least urged the South African regime to open negotiations with accepted leaders of its black majority and to move toward more even-handed policies affecting all its people. Now, Jesse Helms, Barry Goldwater, and Strom Thurmond, strong critics of Carter's African policies, headed key committees in the Republican controlled Senate. Reagan himself was believed to hold similar views. Thus a strong tilt toward the white regime in South Africa could be expected.

In a sophisticated article entitled "South Africa: Strategy for Change," in <u>Foreign Affairs</u> (Winter 1980/81), Chester A. Crocker, an academic who became Assistant Secretary of State for African Affairs, gave notice that he envisaged Southern Africa as both "a changing area" and one of East-West rivalry in which the United States must compete with what he called "our global adversary" if it was to influence and shape that area's destiny.

Crocker maintains that he did not underestimate the potential power of black nationalism to become ultimately a major force within South Africa. However, not surprisingly, he stressed the importance of the political and military white dominance that Prime Minister P.W. Botha was organizing under his own leadership. Crocker thus gave notice that he was determined to work with that force through what he called "constructive engagement" to secure American economic and security interests in Southern Africa.

Crocker hardly mentioned Namibia in his article although the Geneva Conference on Namibia was under way in January 1981 even before the inauguration of the Reagan administration. It had been organized to handle South Africa's charges that the United Nations' bias toward SWAPO made it impossible to enforce the procedures that had been drawn up to implement Security Council Resolution 435. Reagan's refusal even to send an observer to the conference under-cut whatever possibilities it might have had.

Crocker and his staff were far from being unaware, however, of possibilities latent in the Namibian issue. They believed that South African disengagement from Namibia might be bargained aganst the withdrawal of the Cubans from Angola. At least the former seemed more likely if the latter took place.

Crocker opened his initiative late in March 1981, and by the end of the summer, the Contact Group had approved an American plan for negotiations that it was then felt might possibly lead to a final settlement in Namibia. The plan involved three stages: (1) an agreement on basic principles that would protect minority rights after independence; (2) procedures to establish a body that would draw up a constitution; and (3) implementation of these arrangements through a United Nations force. By February 1982, South Africa and SWAPO had agreed on a statement of constitutional principles, and in July 1982, the Contact Group announced that stage one was completed. But by this time, the Cuban issue dominated all discussions.

On September 12, 1982, President Reagan sent a personal letter to African heads of state expressing his own commitment to the linkage principle. It precipitated a bitter diplomatic struggle. The Front Line States rejected the notion of linkage and the Angolans launched wide-ranging efforts to swing African and Eastern opinion behind support for a continued Cuban presence in Angola. Paradoxically, the Cubans probably became still more entrenched in Angola because of the reverberations from the linkage proposal. At least the Americans failed at that point to indicate any official support for UNITA, although that had seemed possible at one time.

The key to the policies directed by Crocker and his deputy, Frank Wisner, has been their belief that Soviet military aggression in Southern Africa will increase and, less convincingly, that Cuban forces in Angola are its focal point. Speaking in Munich on November 9, 1983, Wisner described American policy toward Namibia in simple--indeed oversimplified--terms. He endorsed Resolution 435 as "the best, indeed the only way of obtaining" Namibian independence. In the American view, however, this goal was linked in turn to protecting the security of South Africa itself by removing the Cuban troops from Angola.

To many observers the argument is flawed by its failure to recognize both South Africa's massive military strength, acknowledged by Crocker himself, and by the apparent need to concentrate the Cubans on supporting the MPLA government against the substantial forces and military acumen of its rival UNITA. Though based in the southern part of Angola where its ethnic roots exist, UNITA, well supplied with South African arms, has been able to launch attacks against MPLA facilities in areas well beyond that base.

Questions may be raised as to how the presence of Cuban troops in Angola most affects American policy in Africa. Is the fact of having Cuban troops there of greatest concern for policies toward Namibia and South Africa? Or does the presence of Cuban troops relate more to policies in middle Africa, falling within the broad dimensions of American-Soviet rivalry within that continent? Or is the issue an extension of the long continued tension over Cuba's proximity to the United States, and its influence in other nearby island territories such as Grenada? All these factors may well interrelate to cause the Cuban issue to appear more threatening than any one aspect of the situation might suggest. At least the Reagan administration tried twice, although unsuccessfully, to abrogate the Clark amendment which would remove its restraints on the use of American troops in Angola.

By placing the security of South Africa so firmly in the center of American policy in Southern Africa, the United States has played into the hands of the Botha administration. Not surprisingly, the two regimes agree in their distaste for the Marxist orientation of the governments in both Angola and Mozambique. That orientation has led to American nonrecognition of the MPLA regime in Angola, and temporarily, to the withdrawal of the American ambassador from Mozambique following a dispute over the presence of CIA personnel.

From the South African point of view, however, the danger posed by these two regimes was their hospitality to the exiled African National Congress, the long established standard bearer of African nationalism dedicated to turning South Africa into a non-racial state.

The United States lent a supportive hand to South Africa's negotiations with Mozambique. The result was the N'komati Accord early in March 1984 pledging that each side would refrain from providing sanctuary and aid to the opponents of the other. Mozambique lived up to its pledge and ejected all but a very few active members of the ANC. Combined with a comparable earlier agreement between South Africa and Swaziland, which was publicized only subsequently, the N'komati Accord has noticeably hurt the ANC although not in any sense irreparably. But despite South Africa's pledge under the Accord to help to restrain the Mozambique Resistance Movement (MNR, also known as RENAMO), the latter's devastating attacks inside Mozambique continue, at least once with South African aid.

In an unusually long and comprehensive interview with Johnathan Steele and Victoria Brittain, printed in The Guardian (London) on July 20, 1984, Crocker claimed that the United States had "helped to define an agenda of change, negotiations and development" within which "all the major players" in Southern Africa were participating. Citing, particularly, the N'komati Accord between Mozambique and South Africa, he maintained that "the illusion that armed struggle will solve South Africa's problems has been dealt a body blow."

As for change inside South Africa, Crocker claimed in an earlier interview printed in the airmail edition of The Star (Johannesburg) of June 25, 1984, that "it is already under way" although he admitted that it had not led as yet to results "satisfactory to any of us, you or me." Challenged to describe "specific proposals" that Americans were making to help the South

Africans to "formulate a consistent programme of action
for change," Crocker first mentioned channelling funds
"directly" to black South Africans "to promote black
advancement particularly in the field of education."
In the second place, Crocker took credit for encouraging
"the constructive involvement" of American and other
firms in "removing racism from the economy and the
job market," presumably through the Sullivan principles.
The Republican administration, however, had vigorously
opposed in 1983 a Democratic proposal to impose penalties
under the Export Administration Act on American firms
that did not adhere to those principles.[2] The final
point made rather ambiguously by Crocker in his interview
in The Star was that there were "limits" to the American
relationship with South Africa "in the absence of significant movement away from a system that is based
fundamentally on legally entrenched racism."

Challenged to estimate whether the Mozambique-South
Africa agreement had put "the liberation movements"
on the defensive, and to comment on the future for
SWAPO and the ANC, Crocker made a sharp distinction
between the two organizations. SWAPO, he emphasized,
was an important party to the Namibian negotiations
and had support from the Front Line States and "others
as well, internationally." The ANC, he suggested,
was like "other exile movements such as the Pan
Africanist Congress," and thus apparently to be disre-
garded in any negotiations.

This offhand attitude toward the ANC, the oldest
and most influential exiled movement in South Africa,
seems unfortunately to be characteristic of the attitude
of the Reagan administration. It was challenged during
the 1983 hearings in the Subcommittee on Africa referred
to earlier, and more particularly and in detail in
a substantial scholarly article by Professor Thomas
G. Karis of City University, New York, entitled
"Revolution in the Making: Black Politics in South

Africa," in the Winter 1983-84 issue of Foreign Affairs
(pp. 378-406).

Professor Karis pointed out that the African National
Congress "has become a well-organized liberation movement
with wide-ranging international connections" and is
"now enjoying a broad-based resurgence of support for
its program of resistance to the white South African
government." Although its mobility within Southern
Africa has undoubtedly been hurt by the implementation
of the N'komati Accord, one result seems to have been
to reinforce its links with and bases in other countries
in Southern Africa and to strengthen those within South
Africa itself. This underestimation of the importance
of the African National Congress in the current South
African situation may be one of the Reagan
administration's more important misjudgements.

The counter side of the Reagan administration's
downplaying the role of the African National Congress
is its conviction that, as Wisner stated in the
discussion in the Subcommittee on Africa on September
14, 1983, (p.99), "revolutionary change is under way
in South Africa." He hastily added that, of course,
if repression continued, it would naturally be verbally
condemned. But when Howard Wolpe, chairman of the
Subcommittee, asked why that condemnation should be
taken seriously when at the same time the United States
was moving toward "an expanded closer relationship,"
there was no reply.

On June 23, 1984, Lawrence S. Eagleburger, Under
Secretary of State for Political Affairs, delivered
a comprehensive speech at the National Conference of
Editorial Writers in San Francisco. In its course,
he maintained that "we stand against injustice, and
therefore must reject the legal and political premises
and consequences of apartheid." Going still further,
he declared that "by one means or another, South Africa's
domestic racial system will be changed," but without

specifying in what ways, and whether they would improve the conditions and opportunities of South Africa's huge African majority.

Eagleburger also declared that American and South African interests were "best served by encouraging the change that is now under way in South Africa." He presumably meant the representation being provided the Coloured and Indians under the new constitution which he said it would be "arrogance" to disregard. He made no mention, however, of the fact that both the Coloured and Indian chambers are strictly limited in their actions and effect. Under the new constitution, they may deal with matters affecting their own communities, but on any issue of general concern, all three chambers vote together thereby affording the white majority ultimate control. Moreover, the fact that Prime Minister Botha has become President Botha with a guaranteed five-year term and enhanced authority has further tipped the balance toward continued white administrative control.

What needs to be faced by the United States, regardless of which party is in power, is that there has been little, if any genuine relaxation of the paraphernalia of restrictions on the lives of peoples of color in South Africa. Moreover, there has been a progressive and devastating denationalization of South Africa's African population which despite recent assurances of modifications has done much harm and still threatens more to the African citizens in that country.

On May 21, 1985, South African commandos were intercepted by Angolan security forces in that country's oil rich northern enclave, Cabinda, where the United States Gulf Oil has long operated an important oil refinery. Just under a month later, the commandos attacked South Africa's democratic and unprotected neighbor, Botswana, in a predawn raid on its capital city, Gaborone, ostensibly seeking African National

Congress personnel but in fact killing at least a dozen
South African civilian exiles and refugees.

The United States withdrew Ambassador Herman Nickel
in protest, both against these actions and South Africa's
refusal to apologize for what Botswana's President
called a "bloodcurdling act of murder of defenseless
civilians." This American action raises the question
of when will the United States also formally condemn
the South African government's arbitrary arrests and
imprisonment of its opponents and critics, and particularly its extensive use of torture. Moreover, the
forcible removal and resettlement of whole African
communities that have long had legal rights to where
they live is more than reason enough to protest in
ways the South African government can hardly ignore.
Unfortunately, one is left with words rather than deeds,
and even the words rarely ring true.

What is needed is a consistent policy in Southern
Africa supported by both American political parties
and worked out in conjunction with our Western allies
and with the SADCC countries and South Africa itself.
The Namibian issue must ultimately be settled by its
own people, SWAPO, the United Nations, and South Africa.
How much better it would be if the United States would
reconsider its insistence on Cuban troop withdrawal
from Angola (they have long been north of the line
originally proposed) and encourage the parties most
concerned to work out their own modus vivendi.
Otherwise, one fears still greater violence and little
change except more suffering by those who have never
known much else.

The major problem for Southern Africa is clearly
South Africa itself with its unacceptable racial policy
on the one hand and its dominant military power on
the other. There is always the danger that its military
and police power will be used to block internal or
external policies that seem to threaten Afrikaner

supremacy at home or its own explicit hegemony within the region.

There seem only two possibilities of securing basic change in the structure and practices that result from apartheid and all that flows from the principle of racial domination. One is by internal violence, perhaps supported by some external powers. The other is by international pressure backed up by whatever sanctions are necessary to be effective. If the United States would be willing to take the lead in organizing such pressures, either through a revival of the former Contact Group working with the Front Line States, there would seem some possibilities of success. At least, it seems worth trying in order to forestall still greater violence and suffering within Southern Africa and South Africa itself.

NOTES

1. "The U.S. and Africa: Victory for Diplomacy," Foreign Affairs: America and the World, 1980, pp. 648-666.

2. Hearing on the Internal Political Situation in South Africa in the Subcommittee on Africa, House of Representatives, September 14, 1983, pp. 82ff.

CHAPTER FOUR
CAN SADCC SUCCEED?

In Southern Africa, two conflicting concepts of regional organization are pitted against each other; that of the Southern African Development Coordination Conference (SADCC), linking nine majority ruled independent states, and the South African concept of a "constellation of states" dominated by South Africa itself. Their inter- actions and their outcomes have far reaching national and international implications. This is not only because of the region's rich mineral resources and its strategic position at the foot of the African continent, but also because of the contrast in the concepts of rule and human values underlying each side.

SADCC was formally established on April 1, 1980, after years of planning and preparation. Its avowed aims are to develop the self-sufficiency of its nine members by joint arrangements aided, where possible, by international agencies and foreign governments and to reduce their economic dependence on their apartheid neighbor, as well as in general.

The core of SADCC is its basic nucleus of the Front Line States--Angola, Botswana, Mozambique, Tanzania,

Zambia, and Zimbabwe--whose cohesion was forged in the struggle for the latter's independence, achieved in 1980. They continue to negotiate with outside powers, particularly with members of the former Contact Group --Britain, France, West Germany, Canada, and the United States--over Namibian independence. They also maintain continuing but unofficial relations with two Southern African liberation movements: the African National Congress (ANC), the long established, though exiled, standard bearer of African nationalism in South Africa, and the South West Africa People's Organization (SWAPO), which is widely accepted internationally as the core of the future national government of Namibia, the last non-independent territory in Africa, which is still controlled by South Africa.

In addition to their joint international activities, each of the six Front Line States and the three other SADCC members--Lesotho, Malawi, and Swaziland--which signed the Lusaka Declaration at the same time as the six states listed above, acts as promoter and coordinator for a chosen field of special importance to SADCC: Angola, energy; Botswana, crop research and animal control; Lesotho, soil conservation and land utilization; Malawi, fisheries, wild life and forests; Mozambique, transport and communications; Swaziland, manpower development; Tanzania, industrial development; Zambia, mining and development funding; and Zimbabwe, food security and printing of banknotes. Their efforts are coordinated through regular meetings of the Standing Committee of Officials made up of Permanent Secretaries, and the Council of Ministers; the Secretariat which is housed in Botswana, where President Masire is the SADCC chairman; and the Summit, the meetings of the top political personnel from each SADCC country, which provides its ultimate authority and cohesion.

SADCC holds a variety of meetings, some for its own exchanges, and some to discuss with national and

international organizations the progress its members
are making in their different fields, and the need
for their support. Malawi hosted a major SADCC meeting
in November 1981, and Lesotho another large conference
in January 1983. At both meetings, concern was openly
voiced at South Africa's continuous destabilization
tactics. It was followed by a Heads of State conference
in Maputo, Mozambique, which ended on July 11, 1983,
with a strong plea to Western governments to pressure
South Africa to end its military actions against SADCC
states, in particular Angola. Despite setbacks described
later, the fifth Summit, held in Gaborone, Botswana,
on July 6, 1984, presented an impressive united front.

The second form of regional organization within
Southern Africa is clearly controlled by South Africa,
and designed to support its national purpose of regional
domination. On November 22, 1979, shortly before SADCC
itself was formally established, Prime Minister P.W.
Botha, in a speech to a group of businessmen at Carleton
Center, Johannesburg, spoke of a "constellation of
states" bound closely to South Africa by "joint planning
and action, as well as the pooling of resources."
The "constellation" he envisaged at that time, was
to include Bishop Muzorewa's Rhodesia, and South Africa's
associates in the Southern African Customs
Union--Botswana, Lesotho, and Swaziland--as well as
its own four so-called "independent" homelands: Transkei,
Bophuthatswana, Venda and Ciskei. The rapid transition
of Rhodesia to Zimbabwe, however, and the sharp refusal
of Botswana, in particular, reduced its dimensions
at that time to the units inside South Africa's own
internationally accepted borders.

These initial rebuffs in no sense discouraged the
South African government from pursuing its objective
of developing by one means or another its own close
links with majority ruled Southern African states.
In 1982, in an apparent effort to gain favor with the

Swazi monarchy and, at the same time, to reduce the number of Africans possessing South African citizenship (which, it long maintained, is lost by all Africans of the same ethnic persuasion of so-called "independent" homelands), the South African government attempted to transfer to Swaziland both the KaNgwane homeland and the Ingwavuma strip of Kwa-Zulu, neither of which homelands has accepted "independence." Although the South African Appeal Court subsequently ruled the measure invalid, it seems possible that the South African government may again attempt that or some similar land transfer to Swaziland's advantage. In any case, the attraction of the possibility appears to have persuaded the Swazi government to enter into a secret agreement with South Africa at that time which bears some similarity to the latter's original conception of its "constellation of states."

Nonetheless, Southern Africa remains divided between white controlled apartheid South Africa and most of its majority ruled neighbors, the more so because the relations between the two groups have been embittered by overt violence. Accusing the SADCC states of providing bases for the ANC, whose avowed objective is to establish a non-racial regime in the Republic, South African forces on the night of December 9, 1982, launched a devastating attack from the air on Maseru, the capital of landlocked Lesotho, "with barbaric ferocity," to quote the Commonwealth Secretary-General. At the same time, South Africa was involved in the sabotage of some forty-three oil storage tanks at Beira harbor on whose contents Zimbabwe was depending for its fuel supplies.

There have also been constant raids by the South African army into Angola, coupled with logistic support for Jonas Savimbi's UNITA in its anti-MPLA activities. These raids have crippled that country's railways and ports, thereby seriously hampering Angola's contribution to SADCC's energy resources, although the abundant oil which only it possesses is not now appropriate for existing refineries in other SADCC states (see section below on energy).

Early in 1984, however, the United States sponsored a shaky agreement between the two countries in the interest of opening the way for the long delayed movement toward Namibian independence. The American insistence, however, on linking the withdrawal of Cuban troops from Angola to that of the South African army is a barrier not yet overcome.

On the other side of the continent, South Africa long supplied the Mozambique Resistance Movement (also known as RENAMO), with arms and expertise for its devastating attacks within Mozambique and its sabotage of SADCC's vital transport links to its ocean ports, Nacala, Beira and Maputo.

Here again, 1984 promised major changes through the N'komati non-agression pact signed on March 16, between South Africa and Mozambique, under which each government pledged that it would no longer provide sanctuary and support for the organizations attacking the other state: the ANC on the one side, and the MNR on the other.

South Africa's new political drive to enter into self-restraining agreements with states like Mozambique, which it had previously regarded as a dangerous source of subversion because of its socialist philosophy and its relations, however tenuous, with the Soviet Union and the Eastern Bloc, appeared to be a well founded tactic to curb and possibly destroy what had been a particularly useful center in Southern Africa for the ANC. In February 1981, a brutal attack on unarmed ANC houses in Maputo's adjoining port, Matola, had done little to curb the numbers of ANC personnel living in, or passing through Mozambique, but the N'komati Accord placed the burden of controlling their numbers and activities on the Mozambique government itself, a responsibility it quickly fulfilled, not because it wished to do so but because of the heavy toll it was suffering from MNR attacks. Time has proved, however, that South Africa is unwilling, or possibly incapable of implementing the necessary restrictions on that body to curb its continuing devastation throughout much of Mozambique.

Shortly after the N'komati Accord was announced, Swaziland made it public that it had entered into a similar agreement with South Africa two years earlier. After succeeding with Mozambique, South Africa then turned its attention to Lesotho and Botswana. Both refused to enter into N'komati-type agreements but the pressure on Lesotho, which is embedded within South African territory and greatly dependent upon that country for jobs for its migrant workers as well as for supplies, is particularly difficult to resist. SADCC leaders at their July 1984 Summit urged it to refrain, however, maintaining that whatever the force of circumstances facing Mozambique, other SADCC members did not need to enter into such arrangements. At the same time, the seven leaders at the Summit (Presidents Don Santos of Angola, and Banda of Malawi did not attend) strongly condemned the South African government's actions.

Regardless of the strains in their relations with South Africa, the SADCC states have no illusions regarding their ability to cut their economic ties to that country, however much they may desire to do so. Despite fluctuating prices for gold, which provides the largest source of its government's tax revenues, low returns for other mineral exports, and severe losses to its maize crop due to drought, South Africa's mature economy is basically strong and inevitably overshadows those of the SADCC states. Their minerals are also suffering from low prices especially Zambia's copper, Botswana's diamonds, and Zimbabwe's manganese, while

the drought had affected their crops, leading to near
famine conditions in Mozambique and also, temporarily,
in parts of Zimbabwe's Matabeleland thereby contributing
to its serious unrest. Only Zimbabwe has even a nascent
industrial structure.

Moreover, the higher costs of imports from industrial
states has led to hardships both in the rural and the
urban areas of the SADCC states. They are redoubling
their efforts, therefore, to gain more self-sufficiency.

As SADCC leaders have recognized from the beginning,
transport and communications are the key factors in
achieving their goal of reducing dependence on South
Africa, first by overcoming the dislocations caused
by Ian Smith's Rhodesian UDI, and then by tackling
the more serious problems arising from their colonial
heritage of boundaries which have led to more landlocked
states in Africa than exist on any other continent.
Six of these landlocked states are SADCC members.
Their objective has been to restore alternative transport
routes and harbors to previous levels of operation
and to improve their efficiency in order to take as
much advantage as possible of the ocean ports of the
three other members: Tanzania, Mozambique and Angola.

Already in the sixties, Zambia, fearing correctly
that Ian Smith's UDI might result in blocking its main
outlet to South Africa over the Victoria Falls Bridge,
began to develop new communication links with Tanzania.
The Dar-es-Salaam pipeline to the Copper Belt opened
in 1968, the Great North East Road in the early
seventies, and the Chinese-built Tazara Railway from
Dar-es-Salaam to Zambia'a Kapiri Mposhi in 1975. The
latter's roadbed and rolling stock need costly repairs,
however, for which the EEC agreed to provide aid.
The entry to Dar harbor needs widening and deepening
to handle its ocean shipping more efficiently. In
the West, the Benguela Railway runs only within Angola
and is subject to harrassment by UNITA. There is no
direct connection, therefore, between Zambia and Angola's

ports, and no plans to make it possible at least until a settlement is reached over Namibia.

Mozambique's three ports--Nacala, Beira, and Maputo-- have long histories of serving Malawi and Rhodesia. Malawi is most closely linked to Nacala, Mozambique's best deep water and container port, but the twenty year old railway bed is in very poor condition and there is no communication line between Malawi and Nacala to provide information on the frequent breakdowns. The two hundred kilometers nearest the port are said to be in the worst condition and Mozambique staff, supported by Canadian soft loans and Portuguese commercial export credits, are working on the reconstruction.

To do the whole line, which the French are aiding, is expected to take ten or more years. In the meantime, Nacala harbor itself is slated for development so that it can off-load large ships and transfer their cargo to smaller ones that can use the small harbors in the region. Under such circumstances, and when Nacala harbor is full, Malawi traffic can be sent to Beira on a cut-off spur shortly before Nacala itself, when it is open again after repairs to MNR sabotage. Zambia will also be able to send traffic by these routes in an emergency, but it would first have to traverse Malawi where Canadian aid has completed a railway line from the capital, Lilongwe, up to the Zambian border.

As far as Zimbabwe is concerned, Mozambique and not South Africa is its traditional and more cost efficient outlet. As late as 1972, seventy-five percent of all of Rhodesia's outside traffic went via Mozambique ports and much of the twenty-five percent going to South Africa was internal trade rather than goods for export. Two factors changed this pattern. The Retenga Beit Bridge railway was completed providing Rhodesia with a second and more efficient route through South Africa than the historic one through Botswana and Mafeking; and in March 1976, Mozambique closed its border as a sanction against Ian Smith's regime, adversely affecting Rhodesia but Zambia still more seriously.

Zimbabwe's independence led to efforts to reduce what had become virtually complete dependence on South African routes and ports. In the second half of 1981, 53.2 percent of its external trade went via Beira or Maputo, according to statistics of the Zimbabwe Ministry of Transport, despite periodic sabotage of the transport lines. The greatest damage was caused in October 1981 by sabotage of the bridge over the Pungwe River on the way to Beira harbor. The road bridge was destroyed permanently but the oil pipeline attached to it survived and is now buried, though not deeply, under the water. A mid-1982 agreement with Lonrho which owns the pipeline has enabled Zimbabwe to get its diesel fuel and gasoline direct from the tankers when the lines are intact. Zimbabwean troops patrol the line but sabotage is difficult to prevent.

It is widely believed that the bridge sabotage was caused by the MNR aided by South African equipment and advice but that the sabotage of Beira harbor's marker buoys a month later required a higher degree of sophistication leading to rumors it had been carried out by South African frogmen. Subsequently, as already noted, South African saboteurs participated in the attack on the oil storage tanks at Beira harbor.

Zimbabwe has experienced a steadily increasing demand for rail transport since independence, both for its export trade and for passengers and has invested heavily in refurbishing its old equipment and buying new locomotives. Difficulties caused when South African Railways cancelled its long standing agreement to lease Zimbabwean Railways twenty-five locomotives, which additionally were kept constantly overhauled, were subsequently overcome by more South African flexibility and a substantial local program of refurbishing Zimbabwe's existing locomotives. Additional steam locomotives have been purchased in Canada and the United States, and also electric locomotives from Western Europe for the HarareGwelo line which is being electrified. Local service on equipment is now available and Zimbabwe can also respond to requests for rolling stock from Zambia and Mozambique as well as for itself.

A major constraint on the railways, as in so many other areas, however, is the loss of skilled manpower through retirement, wage restraints, and emigration. Until there is a great increase in the number of Zimbabweans with essential skills, that country must bring in technicians and artisans from outside, for example from India, who serve on a contract basis. This need for more industrial and technical skills is pervasive throughout the SADCC states.

Another problem is the steep gradients on the route from Zimbabwe's capital, Harare, to Beira which make it one of the most expensive lines in Southern Africa, thereby affecting government financing, consumer prices, and investment. Instead of sending its bulk cargoes to Beira harbor, as in pre-war days, Zimbabwe tends to restrict that route to its less bulky and more valuable cargoes like asbestos and refined chrome. Cotton, maize, tobacco, and especially coal were generally shipped via Maputo, when, as is now rare, the lines were open. South African ports with their advanced equipment and greater efficiency continue to be used when necessary or the advantages are manifest.

For the SADCC states, however, Beira harbor remains an essential outlet and its rehabilitation was one of the most advanced of SADCC projects by mid-1983. The Netherlands, which provided temporary buoys after the 1981 sabotage, replaced them with new ones in June 1982, and reinforcement of the port's badly corroded foundations has been proceeding with funds similarly provided by that country. There are plans, too, to change the basic mode of operation. Currently, rail cars go directly to the ships to be unloaded, often causing long delays while awaiting the ship's arrival, or for the unloading of the cars ahead. The new system will be to unload the rail cars at a warehouse where cargoes can be sorted and then transferred to the ships by tractor trailers, thereby reducing the turn-around time for rail stock, and increasing flexibility in loading procedures. In the meantime, Mozambique's ports were reported to be handling about half the rail transport from Zimbabwe and Malawi by the beginning of 1983, and some mineral exports from Zambia and even Zaire. It had been assumed that the N'komati Accord would make it possible for Zimbabwe to ship more of its goods safely to Beira and Maputo than had been the case for some time before, but this seems not yet to be true.

Mozambique, naturally, has a key role in regional transport and communications and is the site of the first permanent SADCC institution: The Southern African Transport and Communications Commission (SATCC). Originally housed on the second floor of the massive Maputo railway station which is next to its well equipped port, the Commission has broad jurisdiction in all forms of transport and communications but focuses most of its attention on rail transport and on port connections with sea transport. Its first priority is to identify what it calls "bundles of transport links" with each port, and thereafter to stimulate cooperation between the national transport agencies that administer their parts of the "bundles." The Commission also acts as a coordinating center for offers of international assistance needed to rehabilitate existing transport routes.

The Transport Commission can receive and manage funds itself although it is more usual for international funds to be channelled directly to the countries in which the projects are physically located. SATCC is responsible for determining the degree of priority

each project deserves. But no project can be presented
to a donor as a SADCC project until the Council of
Ministers has accepted it on the recommendation of
the Commission as a priority project in the Lusaka
Plan of Action. Some donors feel it would be helpful
if the Commission itself were empowered to assign
priorities among programs within the Plan of Action.

The Scandinavian countries have made themselves
responsible for meeting most of the salaries and expenses
of the Commission's own secretarial and technical
personnel. The latter are responsible for identifying
those transport lines that have genuine regional
significance, and identifying what needs to be done
to increase their efficiency. The Commission usually
acts as liaison between the states involved in a
particular project.

We were told by Commission officials in mid-1982
that there had been little difficulty in securing
necessary support for identified and approved projects
and that the funds had already been transferred to
the relevant parties. By the start of 1983, SATCC
could report on progress or completion of twenty-seven
communication projects, costing some $181 million.
In mid-1984, SATCC reported on 115 projects concerned
with a wide variety of activities: port rehabilitation,
road and rail upgrading, civil aviation and
telecommunications. The total estimated cost was $2,935
million of which $1,349 million had been secured or
was under negotiation.

A major bottleneck in getting SADCC goods in and
out of Mozambique's ports, as Pedro Figueiredo of the
SATCC pointed out in the January, 1983, issue of African
Business (p.61), is poor line-of-rail communications.
SATCC is therefore giving attention also to telecommuni-
cation projects and particularly to providing more
satellite earth stations throughout SADCC countries.
Several of them already have at least one station

directed to either the Atlantic or the Indian Ocean satellite. Mozambique expects two more to be operational in 1984, the one for Beira to be financed by the Kuwait Fund; Angola and Tanzania their second; and Lesotho, Zimbabwe, and Swaziland their first, the latter through Canadian financing. The EEC is paying for the Zimbabwe earth station. Botswana's standard B earth station installation at Kgale is said to be Africa's most modern telecommunication system although its integral digital telecommunication network and microwave links are not yet completed.

For reliable communication that will avoid messages passing through South Africa, a SADCC microwave network is needed. The Scandinavian countries are already financing direct links between Zimbabwe, Botswana, and Zambia; Zimbabwe's should be ready in 1985. The EEC has agreed to finance the Malawi-Tanzania microwave link-up. Mozambique, unfortunately, has no microwave network and despite study and implementation funds from Sweden and Italy, the estimate is that it will cost $108 million, and not be ready for use before 1989 at the earliest. All such systems are expected to operate as commercial entities, and are regularly monitored through it's headquarters in Gaborone, which was set up in 1981 by Zimbabwe, Zambia, Swaziland, Malawi, and Botswana.

Air links between SADCC countries and beyond are still limited but expanding. There are a few direct flights between Lusaka and Harare, and on to Gaborone, but generally there is heavy dependence on South African airports as transfer points. Air Zimbabwe, SADCC's major carrier, is one of the few airlines in Africa that can carry out repairs on its own aircraft without outside help. It will also do so for aircraft belonging to other SADCC states. Air Zimbabwe is also prepared to help to train staff for other SADCC airfleets.

Among their many needs, SADCC countries naturally place food security high. There is deep concern both nationally and internationally at the growing disparity in developing countries between their food production and their needs. In 1981, a World Bank staff report entitled <u>Accelerated Development in Sub-Saharan Africa: An Agenda For Action</u> compared the striking advances in education, life expectancy, roads, ports, cities, and new industries in Africa with what it called the "consistent bias" against agriculture in price, taxes, and exchange-rate policies that have discouraged local production and greatly increased local food needs. Subsequently, Professor Carl Eicher, an outstanding expert in this field, pointed out in an article in <u>Foreign Affairs</u> (October, 1982) that donor states with food surpluses have tended to use them for aid to developing countries and, by encouraging African governments to concentrate on saleable export goods rather than on agriculture, have intensified this bias.

Only Zimbabwe, the coordinator in this field, has a well established commercial agriculture which under the best conditions of abundant harvests (not known generally since 1981), and of satisfactory transport and payment arrangements can meet the needs of its neighbors, as South Africa's traditional surpluses, often sold below domestic prices, have so often done in the past. But Zimbabwe has confronted a unique problem in expanding its output since the productivity of its large white-owned farms normally far outstrips that of its peasant cultivators. In 1985, however, the latter produced a bumper harvest of particular psychological importance since the war for independence was to a considerable degree fought over landholding, and more equitable land ownership is a basic government pledge.

The main foodstuffs consumed in the SADCC region are maize, wheat, sorghum and, to a lesser extent, animal products. The 1980 estimates of the existing food situation within the SADCC group indicated that the net availability from both local and imported sources only met about ninety percent of its needs. There was thus a ten percent shortfall to be made up at that time and since then a great deal more as the drought has continued while there has been no let up in the increase in population every year.

In line with SADCC's general approach, a series of feasibility studies financed by different donors have been undertaken by outside consultancies on such related subjects as food reserve systems, post harvest food loss reduction schemes, regional food processing, food marketing, and food aid projects to ascertain possible options which the SADCC states could individually and collectively pursue. These reports have been discussed at meetings of agricultural specialists from those SADCC countries particularly interested in that topic. After a particular option has been chosen, the original or another consultancy is selected to draw up detailed proposals for how it should be carried out.

At the July 1982 Summit meeting in Gaborone, ministers were instructed to complete a food security sufficiency scheme for the region for the international conference in Maseru, Lesotho, in January, 1983. Part of the basic plan was that each SADCC state should stock at least three months supply of one or two staple commodities. A number of donors have agreed to help them meet this goal.

The Food Security project farthest advanced by mid-1982 was the Early Warning System whose potentialities had been demonstrated in Tanzania by an agricultural specialist, Steve Lombard. He set up an information system using local volunteers to monitor daily rainfall, the key factor in the growth of maize, the basic food crop, and to transmit the

information weekly by pre-paid postcards to a central
point for analysis. In this way, it would be possible
to determine where the crops were abundant and which
areas were in danger of failure.

The obvious purpose was to forestall the danger
of famine in particular areas by moving surplus supplies
to them or, where these were lacking, to arrange in
good time for external supplies to be imported to meet
the need. The system worked well, but unfortunately
the information was not transmitted to the proper
authorities until Lombard himself went to President
Nyerere. By then some disaster areas had developed
and Lombard's contract was terminated. He is now based
in Zimbabwe and travels widely to expand the use of
the system throughout the SADCC region. The Food and
Agriculture Organization (FAO) finances the broad
feasibility study that he is carrying out as he had
worked under their auspices in Tanzania.

USAID has funded another aspect of the food security
program: technical assistance for all agrarian issues.
This program involves three consultative technical
committees, each one composed of the national directors
of the three interrelated sectors of agricultural administration: research, extension services, and marketing
and economics. Funding permits each committee to meet
annually to identify activities, gaps, and needs in
each area, thus making possible a constant updating
of agrarian developments throughout the SADCC region.

By 1984, the prolonged drought, coupled with rapid
population growth, resulted in the largest food deficit
in the world in the region of which the SADCC group
of countries were a part. Between 1979 and 1981, the
region had been 95 percent self-sufficient in home-grown
food, yet it is estimated that without drastic changes,
the self-sufficiency level will have dropped by 1990
to eighty percent. To limit, and perhaps avoid so
drastic a development, Senator Denis Norman, Zimbabwe's
then Minister of Agriculture, pointed out at the Common-

wealth Institute Conference in July, 1984, the need to enlarge, where possible, the area used for crop production, and to make more extensive use of irrigation to compensate ·for what he called the "varied and erratic nature" of the rainfall in the region.

Above all, Senator Norman urged training and education for the large proportion of the region's population which is still farming. By lifting their production above subsistence level, they might not only help to meet the food needs of their countries but also be dissuaded from moving to the towns. He also urged "immediate" attention to expanding market and storage depots and onward distribution systems to ensure that over-production in an area is not wasted, and stressed the importance of adequate pricing of rurally produced crops.

In another approach to improving agricultural outputs, Botswana had earlier been asked to make contact on SADCC's behalf with the International Crops Research Institution for Semi-Arid Tropics (ICRISAT) sited at Hyderabad in India, which specializes in ground nuts, pigeon peas, and sorghum, in the hope that it would establish a local Southern African station. In addition to recommending better coordination between SADCC's existing research stations and international agencies, ICRISAT has also set up a regional sorghum and maize research program at Matopos, Zimbabwe.

Botswana is making its own creative contribution to SADCC in the field of animal husbandry. Beef provides its major export to the EEC market, to which its entry was guaranteed during the lifetime of Lome II, and then beyond. During the Zimbabwean war Botswana's herds were threatened by foot and mouth disease brought over the border by cattle belonging to Rhodesian refugees. Its experience in freeing itself from this disease by selective fencing and the development of an improved vaccine has aided the general prevention

of animal diseases in the SADCC region. Moreover,
Botswana can not only produce enough foot and mouth
vaccine for its own needs, but through its Gaborone
laboratory is expanding the supply to meet the needs
of other SADCC states.

Veterinary training, which is obviously related,
is provided by Zimbabwe which has already established
a training unit at its University. It also has plans
for a Food Science Department. Together with these
developments and resources from the annual pledging
conferences, there is hope of assuring improved regional
food security, now second only to the emphasis on
regional transport facilities.

Industry and energy are two relatively new but highly
important fields that have been accepted as SADCC areas
of concentration within the limits of the Lusaka
Declaration. Although industry as a SADCC field was
only introduced officially at the 1983 Maseru SADCC
Conference, Tanzania, the responsible country for
industrial development coordination in the region,
was able to report at the July 1984 conference at the
London Commonwealth Institute that there had been
striking success in securing support for the eighty-eight
projects it has proposed. All meet the two basic
criteria for acceptance as SADCC projects: an existing
foreign exchange gap in its funding, and products that
benefit more than one member state. Fifty-five of
its eighty-eight projects were ready for implementation
by that time and thirty-three were ready for studies
prior to implementation. The total cost of the
eighty-eight projects amounted to $843 million of which
$213.3 million had already been confirmed; the remaining
$629.7 million worth of pledges were in various stages
of detailed negotiation.

Projects already under way included nine related
to development or expansion of salt works, two in
Mozambique, five in Tanzania, and one each in Lesotho

and Botswana. Under textiles, there were five knitting projects; one each in Botswana, Lesotho, Malawi, Mozambique, and Zambia; six powerloom projects in the same countries except for Mozambique, but in addition, Tanzania and Swaziland; five polyester yarn projects, two in Tanzania, and one each in Mozambique, Zambia and Zimbabwe; three under wool and mohair: scouring, Lesotho, spinning, Botswana, and blankets, Zimbabwe; and two for textile processing chemicals, Botswana and Tanzania.

Fifteen projects are devoted to tractors and farm implements: three for Tanzania, two for Swaziland, three for Zambia, two for Botswana, two for Lesotho, and one each for Zimbabwe, Angola, and Malawi. There are also four devoted to fertilizers, one in Malawi, and two in Mozambique, one of which is for rehabilitation of the Matola plant destroyed during the 1981 South African attacks on the ANC houses. One is simply listed as phosphate fertilizers. There are also five pulp and paper projects: two for Zimbabwe, and one each for Tanzania, Zambia, and Mozambique, and three for cement, all for Mozambique.

Electrical transmission and distribution equipment projects are still under study as are ten pesticide/insecticide formulation plants, and a number of salt and textile chemical plants, but those already under way demonstrate the practicality of the projects and the wide spread of their distribution.

In the light of their collective resources in oil, coal, gas and hydroelectric power, the SADCC states would seem to be bountifully supplied with all the energy that they can use, but the distribution of these resources and their linkage requirements need complicated arrangements. These have only recently been studied adequately by the Beijer Institute of the Royal Swedish Academy of Sciences. Their detailed findings and analysis were published jointly with the Scandinavian

International African Institute in four volumes late in 1984.

Angola, the responsible country for SADCC's energy program, has large quantities of oil but rarely sells to its SADCC partners partly because of payment difficulties, but more particularly because the three refineries in Mozambique, Tanzania and Zimbabwe are designed for Middle East crude and not for Angolan crude. During the SADCC conference at the Commonwealth Institute in July 1984, Angolan Energy and Petroleum Minister Pedro Van Dusen, who is also chairman of the SADCC energy ministers conference, suggested that in the long run, the other SADCC states will need new refinery capacity and that this could include rebuilding to take Angolan crude. He also stressed the need for hydrocrackers, such as have been proposed for Angola itself, to reduce the over-supply of heavy crude oil and the under production of lighter products. In the meantime, he left open the possibility of exchanging oil for goods to stimulate inter-regional trade.

The UN Development Program has provided $4 million for the regional petroleum center in Luanda, and Canada has allocated $60 million of the $125 million it pledged for the years 1985-1990 at the Lusaka donors conference in February 1984. The bulk of these funds will be used to finance feasibility studies and the implementation of four transmission connection projects: Botswana/Zimbabwe, Botswana/Zambia, Mozambique/Swaziland, and Zambia/Malawi/Tanzania. Negotiations are also under way with Norway for the Mozambique/Zimbabwe interconnection.

In Mr. Van Dusen's view, conversion of coal, of which the SADCC states possess some of the world's largest deposits, particularly in Botswana, is a promising solution to SADCC's goal to be "truly self sufficient in energy by the year 2000." The high transport costs and depressed world demand for coal strongly suggest, in his view, that the reserves should be used locally.

One of the potential problems facing the SADCC countries is that presently nearly eighty percent of current energy consumption comes from biomass, mainly wood and charcoal, reflecting the rural situation of most of the SADCC population, particularly those living at subsistence level. Donors, particularly the EEC, the Netherlands, and Sweden have been attracted by the five wood fuel projects that have been presented to them but investigations are still at an early stage.

Great regional disparities exist in the consumption of energy among the SADCC states ranging from a low per capita figure of about 500 kg for Angola to a high of nearly three times that amount for Swaziland. Projected to the year 2000, energy consumption is expected to increase eighty percent, resulting in a seventy percent increase in biomass consumption. However, industrial development and increased rural to urban migration will mean rapid increases in the use of commercial fuels, especially electricity, coal, and petroleum consumption. Current estimates, however, indicate that SADCC's exploitable energy sources can more than meet the demands that will be put on them.

Promising would seem to be the potential power existing through SADCC's massive water resoures and in particular by tapping the Zambezi River and its subsidiaries. Although the power lines from the huge Cabora Bassa dam on the lower Zambezi in Mozambique presently run only to South Africa, which shared its financing with Portugal, and to Maputo through the South African grid, Mozambique's government has well advanced plans, along with some international donors, to develop a separate direct source of Zambezi power.

The earlier Kariba Dam provides power to both Zimbabwe and Zambia. Each has additional power resources, Zambia through the Kafue dam, built during a time of tension over Rhodesia's UDI, and Zimbabwe through the Wankie thermal power plant. The latter is already at stage two and private firms from Britain, West Germany and other European countries continue to work on its development. There are also ambitious plans to build at least one more dam on the Zambezi while an imaginative, long range proposal envisages a linkage of all the power plants on the Zambezi River to provide power throughout the region. Coupled with massive resources of coal, indications of natural gas off the Tanzanian coast, and also, ultimately, oil from Angola, the SADCC states hope they can reduce their dependence on imports of fossil fuels by expanding their own power resources and thereby developing more balanced economies.

Manpower development is a major SADCC concern for which Swaziland has special responsibility. Manpower development obviously cuts across and has an impact on every other priority area, especially teacher training and educational facilities but also trade, energy, agriculture, transportation and development. It was identified as one of SADCC's ten major strategies at the second Council of Ministers meeting held at Maputo in November 1980. In response to its recommendations, a Regional Training Council was established in 1981 with responsibilities for planning and coordination. It identified six major areas where consulting services were needed: for the sugar industry, and the mining sector but, in particular, in the light of the variety of languages and educational patterns existing among the nine SADCC countries, in health training, teacher training, comparability of educational levels and regional manpower information.

Sensitive to limitations of time and resources, the consulting team for the latter areas focused on four major topics that had not up to that time received detailed attention. These topics were: 1) comparability and compatibility of entry standards between the nine

SADCC states; 2) information on courses of study in the various post-secondary programs and institutions which seemed likely to provide region-wide manpower training services; 3) their levels of compatibility; and 4) institutions or programs of regional or potentially regional significance. Being aware that the SADCC Regional Training Council Secretariat was eliciting information on the latter subject through a questionnaire, the team limited its inquiries to data that the questionnaire seemed unlikely to cover.

The teams' report deals in detail with comparability of credentials based on a review of the educational systems of each of the nine countries, of which the seven English-speaking countries--Botswana, Lesotho, Malawi, Swaziland, Tanzania, Zambia and Zimbabwe--share some common features, and of the two Portuguese-speaking countries--Angola and Mozambique--which also share common features, but ones that differ substantially, however, from those of the first group. Unfortunately, the information available on specialized training in agriculture, veterinary science, industry, transportation and communication, and secondary school training, proved inadequate for effective comparison. While the project remains highly important in terms of long range planning, it is obvious that much more detailed information and study are necessary to underpin programs that are geared to its overall goal.

In the original allocation of SADCC responsibilities, Botswana had agreed to undertake certain secretarial functions and these were supplemented by those performed by the London-based Liaison Committee. The latter consists of all the High Commissioners and Ambassadors of SADCC states that are posted there, or to the EEC in Brussels and of certain additional members who have been concerned with SADCC's progress since its inception and serve in their individual capacities. These individuals are Dr. David Anderson, former Assistant

Secretary-General of the Commonwealth Secretariat and Managing Director of the Commonwealth Fund for Technical Cooperation, Paul Spray of the Catholic Liaison Group, who acts as secretary to the Liaison Committee, and Dr. Reginald Green of Sussex University whose long experience serving in Africa made him a natural choice to be one of the original drafters of SADCC's basic documents. The weekly meetings of the Liaison Committee help to facilitate exchanges of information, and to maintain contact with international agencies. In addition, Tim Sheehy, based in Zimbabwe, travels to reinforce mutual interactions.

The growing administrative burdens of serving SADCC's increasing range of activities soon led to its second formal institution, the nine member Permanent Secretariat, whose establishment was announced in July 1982, at a Summit meeting in Gaborone, Botswana, where its office is sited. Zimbabwe's Ambassador Arthur Blumeris was the original Executive Secretary but since his untimely death, the post has been filled by Dr. Simbarashe Makoni. Dr. Makoni has had unusually wide and varied experience in the Zimbabwe government, first as Deputy Minister of Agriculture, then from 1982-1984 as Minister of Industry and Energy, and from January 1984 as Minister of Youth, Sport, and Culture until he assumed his new post heading the SADCC Secretariat.

The basic principle governing SADCC's pattern of administration is that "SADCC work is national work," to quote Mr. Emang Maphanyane of the Botswana Ministry of Finance, who had served on the temporary Secretariat. With the rare exceptions, therefore, of SATCC and the Secretariat's nine members, the functioning of SADCC organs is basically carried on by officials who already have heavy domestic responsibilities. Increasingly, however, countries that carry particularly active programs have established small specialist Units that deal exclusively with SADCC affairs in the field assigned

to their governments. These Units are assisted by
professionals recruited under technical assistance
agreements. While this arrangement functions relatively
well under current conditions, it seems likely that
SADCC will feel it necessary soon to reconsider and
probably expand its long term staffing arrangements.

SADCC's three major governing bodies are in ascending
order, the Standing Committee of Officials which is
made up of Permanent Secretaries; the Council of
Ministers; and the Summit. The first two meet at least
three times a year and tend to do so at the same time
although this is not required. The Summit, which as
its name indicates, gives final approval to decisions,
is generally attended by the Heads of State or some
Minister with power to commit his government, and thus
confirms each state's political role in SADCC. Many
experienced observers believe that the Summit provides
SADCC's ultimate and essential cohesion.

One necessary key to harmony among SADCC members
is that each shall have a satisfying coordination
responsibility. This has generally not been a problem
but Zambia's inital proposal for the SADCC Development
Bank was received with a noticeable lack of enthusiasm
both by its fellow SADCC states and by donor countries.
Zambia was requested, therefore, by the Council, to
carry out a further and fuller study which would take
into account various other proposals for financial
institutions that had been broached previously, including
the PTA proposal supported by Zambia, which is considered
below. Another proposal which was not accepted was
a veterinary training project presented both by Zambia
and Zimbabwe. Since neither country had observed the
SADCC procedures for bringing a project to the consider-
ation of the Council, neither appears to have been
officially accepted. These two situations, however,
are virtually unique and, under ordinary circumstances,
new proposals are well prepared for presentation to

the Council and are, therefore, almost always accepted.

SADCC is not the only regional organization promoting greater economic interaction between East and Southern African states. After the collapse of the East African Community in 1977, the Economic Commission for Africa, a sub-organization of the Economic and Social Council of the United Nations, established a Multinational Programming and Operational Center (MULPOC) for that area in Lusaka. MULPOC proposed and promoted a treaty for a Preferential Trade Agreement Area (PTA) and in 1978, nine of its most likely seventeen members agreed to negotiate such a treaty. At present, nearly twenty states, including Zimbabwe and the BLS contries (despite their special trade relation with South Africa) have agreed to take advantage of its provisions.

The purpose of PTA is to promote intra-regional trade through negotiated reduction of tariff barriers, a more limited but parallel purpose to one of SADCC's own objectives. Already, in fact, Tanzania and Mozambique had devised an effective system of bilateral trade involving a reciprocal account in each country's central bank, but it is dependent on maintaining relatively equitable flows of trade between the participants. Whether this system might be extended to other SADCC states, or whether the existence of PTA and SADCC with their separate mandates and budgets will provide additional strains on the independent states of Southern Africa remains to be seen.

Another association of interest to the SADCC states is concerned with research in both the social and the natural sciences. In November 1981, the first International Workshop on Research Priorities in Southern Africa was held at the National University of Lesotho with representatives also present from Britain and the United States. One of the most constructive aspects of the meeting was its stress on the need to promote manpower capability in research and training, a major deficiency among the SADCC states which is also being tackled by SADCC itself.

While the SADCC states are thus willing to participate in other country groupings aimed at improving the economic and research potential of the region, they have been careful so far not to divert too much of their energies outside their own extensive responsibilities. Useful as these other efforts may well be, there seems little doubt that for the foreseeable future, SADCC will retain the primary role in sponsoring balanced development and greater economic independence among its nine majority ruled states of the region.

To gain economic support for the facilities they need to aid their efforts to reduce their dependence, especially upon South Africa, the SADCC states naturally turn to the developed states and to international lending organizations like the International Monetary Fund (IMF) and the more recently established African Development Bank (ADB). The latter pledged by far the largest amount at the conference for donors in Maputo, Mozambique, in November 1980, which sought support for SADCC's far reaching needs in transport and communications. The IMF has far greater resources than the ADB, however, and is the major source for debt plagued countries like Zambia which by 1982 ranked eighth among its heaviest borrowers, and had already reached its credit limit, i.e. 450 percent of its quota.

It has been the misfortune of the SADCC states to seek such international aid at a time of world wide recession combined with unexpected monetary crises in countries like Mexico and Brazil which threatened to overwhelm IMF resources. Only after intense negotiations at its annual meeting in September 1982 did several states make the necessary pledges for an increase in the lending authority of IMF, and there are already new, unfulfilled and urgent needs.

SADCC states like Malawi, needing support for agricultural projects with multiple purposes such as its Shire Valley Agricultural Consolidation Project, turn to the International Development Association (IDA), a World Bank association that gives "soft" loans to the poorer countries at no interest and with long grace periods.

USAID was specifically alerted to the needs of SADCC countries through a Congressionally-mandated study, released in March 1979, which identified many of the same restraints affecting Southern African majority ruled states that SADCC itself focuses upon. Of the $100 million projected for FY 1980, forty-three percent was for agriculture and soil conservation. Its largest recipient that year was Zambia, while Malawi got a third of a million for small holder agricultural projects. USAID's regional development officer, Mr. Dale Peiffer, based in Harare, Zimbabwe, works on developing overall plans focused on assisting SADCC's development efforts.

Britain and the United States, in that order, have been Zimbabwe's largest donors. In addition to the more common project aid, American assistance to Zimbabwe has been in part in the form of program aid, which is particularly effective because it is provided in dollars. It thus lessens the outflow of Zimbabwe's scarce foreign currency and, in addition, can be used to purchase goods in the United States which can be sold locally to private industry or to the semi-public sector to replace aged capital equipment, thereby increasing the return.

Individual members of EEC provide their own aid to particular SADCC members either for individual or regional projects. In addition, seven of SADCC's nine members have had a special economic relationship to the Community as a whole through signing Lome Convention I (1976), II (1979), and III (1985) as they became eligible. While the Convention requires its member developing states to stabilize their export prices, and to give privileges to the European market, it also enables them to receive community development aid. Until mid-1982, however, neither Angola nor Mozambique were willing to sign the obligatory Berlin clause acknowledging British, French, and American rights in that city and that it is part of West Germany. They were, therefore, excluded from the Convention and joint EEC economic assistance. Both Mozambique and Angola have now reached an agreement with the EEC on this issue and will, therefore, be eligible to participate in the agreements under Lome Convention III.

Aid from the United States and the EEC is somewhat counterbalanced by the restrictions on imports that these developed countries impose. Zimbabwe would like the United States to admit its sugar more freely and to be given a specific quota for this product. The EEC's common external tariff is a barrier to competition in textiles by all third world states, and this restriction has recently been extended by the new Multi-Fiber Arrangement (MFA). Opportunities to help themselves are thus being denied to developing states.

In determining where aid should go to the SADCC states, various criteria appear to be used. Support for improved transport and communication arangements that benefit the SADCC states is widely accepted as a valid claim on international resources. Help in establishing self-sufficiency in food and other basic requirements can also be well justified as means to insulate them individually and collectively against famine and a constant need for aid but may be less so beyond the point of stabilizing regional needs. In particular areas where the SADCC states can become genuinely competitive with South African exports, or are already so, there seems a good case for enhancing their productivity. Technical advice and support for maximizing efforts in the wide range of subjects in which SADCC states are themselves concentrating, and particularly for manpower development in needed skilled areas of their economies, seem normal international responses from both the public and private sectors to third world needs.

Southern Africa is at a median point between peace and conflict. The South African success in persuading Mozambique to accept the N'komati Accord, and the earlier acceptance of similar arrangements by Swaziland are hardly surprising considering the continuous raids especially on the former by the powerful guerrilla units of the MNR which at least earlier were armed and possibly directed from the Republic. South African pressure to sign similar arrangements has also been directed at Lesotho, and to a much lesser degree at Botswana. Moreover, to persuade them to accept comparable restraints, Zimbabwe and Zambia have also not been wholly free from raids either by the MNR or, more likely, directly from South Africa, which for a while appeared to be capitalizing on local unrest in Matabeland.

South African troops remain in or near Angola's southern section. Namibia is far from free and independent. Is this the time that South Africa, backed tacitly by the Reagan administration, has established the Southern African hegemony which it has so long sought? Has it, indeed, secured a "constellation of states" that is far more impressive than could have been anticipated when it was first proposed?

Or is this a time of transition when the South African government appears to be at its strongest regionally but has failed to establish peace at home? As described in the latter pages of Chapter Two, "Coercive Rule in South Africa," there have been unprecedented continuing demonstrations of hostility toward the South African government and its policies and agents by its own massive black population and their white supporters.

The government's response on July 21, 1985 was to declare a state of emergency, the first since the Sharpeville shootings in 1960. The purpose was to erect a screen behind which the government could make unhampered use of powers it already possessed to silence protests and eliminate their most effective spokesmen.

South Africa is going through a time marked by continued turmoil, as well as by internal and external change. Planning for a more effective role within Southern Africa does not fit well with its own internal disorders. Even though the N'komati Accord appeared to be a major victory, South Africa's inability to stop the MNR from its devastating attacks within Mozambique weakens its position. Looking ahead, both internal and external problems seem inevitably to handicap the South African government in its efforts to achieve stability at home and increased influence within Southern Africa as a whole.

This may well be the time, therefore, for SADCC to double its efforts for regional self-development in the many areas to which its members are committed. Much has already been accomplished but even more remains to be done. SADCC has the leadership, structure, and international support it needs. Its own unity, determination, and cooperative efforts can be expected to provide continued growth and achievements.

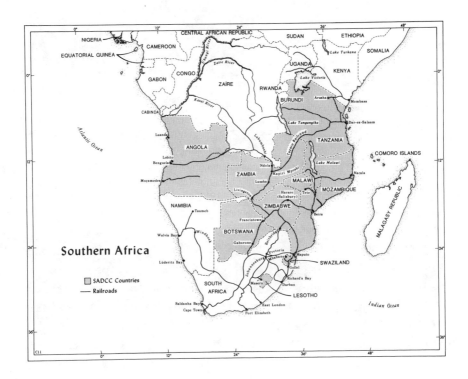

By permission, Indiana University Press, 1985.

CHAPTER FIVE
SOUTHERN AFRICA: A BIBLIOGRAPHIC ESSAY

No African area is so constantly in the headlines as is Southern Africa with its possibilities of great power confrontations and its own explosive issue of black-white conflict over political power. Shaped by geography, history and political action into a distinctive region at the southern end of the African continent, its nine independent states--Angola, Botswana, Lesotho, Malawi, Mozambique, South Africa, Swaziland, Zambia, and Zimbabwe--differ widely in their historical backgrounds, international alignments, ideological sentiments, character of rule, economic strength, and much besides. Forced to interact by propinquity and lines of trade, there are many underlying strains, both internally and between states, that frequently threaten the region's peace and stability. Among them is the future of Namibia, the one non-independent entity in the region. It is still controlled by the Republic of South Africa despite decades of international efforts to bring it to independence.

As described in the preceeding papers, South Africa is by far the strongest, most developed, and most controversial state in Southern Africa. Controlled by its white minority since it achieved independence from Great Britain in 1910, and politically dominated by Afrikaner Nationalists since 1948, South Africa is widely known and criticized for its coercive rule and apartheid policies of racial segregation, particularly of its huge black African majority, but also to a lesser degree of its Coloured (mixed blood) population and Indian minority.

The most distinctive aspect of the government's African segregation program is the homeland, or Bantustan policy through which increasing numbers of blacks are forced into one or another of ten territories, most of which are on the periphery of the country. South Africa itself maintains they are entities separate from the main body of the country but no other state accepts that position. Underdeveloped and overpopulated, the only jobs available to the inhabitants of the homelands are generally as migrants. Because of its significance, there is a separate section devoted to the Bantustan program, and the homelands.

South Africa's strategic position at the foot of the continent, its well developed ports, modern transportation system, and, above all, its almost unparalleled mineral resources have long powered a strong and highly developed economy. Currently, however, South Africa is suffering a recession. Moreover, those members of its African majority who are domiciled in the black townships and who form so large a percentage of the work force in industry and commerce are increasingly restive. Ever larger numbers of these workers are now enrolled in recognized black unions which, as already described, demonstrated their power through a disciplined two day stay-at-home in November 1984 protesting the use of soldiers along with police to crush township protests over living conditions and rents.

Moreover, the introduction of the new constitution which provides representation along with whites for Coloured and Indians, but excludes Africans, has led to ever increasing black protests and unrest, to widespread school boycotts and to a degree of political tension in rural areas that has rarely existed before. While none of this yet offers a dangerous threat to the stability of the South African regime, it inserts new pressures into the total situation in that country which seek increasingly to force substantial changes.

Not surprisingly, an almost endless number of books and articles have been written about South Africa. My first work on its political system, THE POLITICS OF INEQUALITY: SOUTH AFRICA SINCE 1948, published in 1958, sought to provide an overall view based on research between 1948 and 1956. Among the many more specialized books available that no one should overlook is Gail Gerhart's BLACK POWER IN SOUTH AFRICA: THE EVOLUTION OF AN IDEOLOGY. Another basic work is John Dugard's HUMAN RIGHTS AND THE SOUTH AFRICA LEGAL ORDER.

Because situations change so frequently, there is no substitute for following the South African scene through THE NEW YORK TIMES, or THE CHRISTIAN SCIENCE MONITOR, or THE WASHINGTON POST, first class periodicals like AFRICA NEWS and AFRICA REPORT, the weekly AF PRESSCLIPS from the Department of State and, if possible, a good South African newspaper like the airmail edition of THE JOHANNESBURG STAR (weekly). THE MANCHESTER GUARDIAN WEEKLY and THE ECONOMIST, both airmail from England, are very useful in providing distinctive approaches to significant issues.

SOUTH AFRICA

Adam, Heribert, (ed.), SOUTH AFRICA: THE LIMITS OF REFORM POLITICS. Leiden: E.J. Brill, 1984, 115pp.

Biko, Steve, (Millard Arnold, ed.), BLACK CONSCIOUSNESS IN SOUTH AFRICA, New York, Vintage, 1978, 360pp.

Boesak, Allan, BLACK AND REFORMED: APARTHEID, LIBERATION AND THE CALVINIST TRADITION, (Leonard Sweetman, ed.,) Maryknoll, New York, Orbis Books, 1984, 167pp.

Boulle, L.J., CONSTITUTIONAL REFORM AND APARTHEID, New York: St. Martin's, 1984, 270pp.

Carter, Gwendolen M., THE POLITICS OF INEQUALITY: SOUTH AFRICA SINCE 1948, New York, Praeger, 1958, 535pp.

Crapanzano, Vincent, WAITING: THE WHITES OF SOUTH AFRICA, New York, Random House, 1985, 358pp.

de Klerk, W.A., THE PURITANS IN AFRICA: A STORY OF AFRIKANERDOM, London, Collins, 1975, 376pp.

Dugard, C.J.R., HUMAN RIGHTS AND THE SOUTH AFRICAN LEGAL ORDER, Princeton, Princeton University Press, 1978, 470pp.

·Frederickson, George M., WHITE SUPREMACY: A COMPARATIVE STUDY IN AMERICAN AND SOUTH AFRICAN HISTORY, New York, Oxford University Press, 1981.

Gerhart, Gail M., BLACK POWER IN SOUTH AFRICA: THE EVOLUTION OF AN IDEOLOGY, Berkeley, University of California Press, 1978, 364pp.

Goodwin, Joan, AMANDLA: SOUTH AFRICA'S WOMEN: THE QUESTION OF POWER, Africana Publishing Company, New York, 1984, 253pp.

Greenberg, Stanley B., RACE AND STATE IN CAPITALIST DEVELOPMENT: COMPARATIVE PERSPECTIVES, New Haven, Yale University Press, 1980, 489pp.

Hanf, Theodor, et al., SOUTH AFRICA: THE PROSPECTS OF PEACEFUL CHANGE, Bloomington, Indiana University Press, 1981, 492pp.

MacShane, Denis, Martin Plaeet, and David Ward, BLACK WORKERS: THEIR UNIONS AND THE STRUGGLE FOR FREEDOM IN SOUTH AFRICA, Boston, South End Press, 1984, 195pp.

Nolutshungu, Sam C., CHANGING SOUTH AFRICA: POLITICAL CONSIDERATIONS, New York, Africana Publishing Co., 1982, 219pp.

North, James, FREEDOM RISING, Macmillan Publishing Co., New York, 1985, 336pp.

Price, Robert M., and Carl G. Rosberg, THE APARTHEID REGIME: POLITICAL POWER AND RACIAL DOMINATION, Berkeley, Institute of International Studies, University of California, 1980, 376pp.

Slabbert, F. Van Zyl and David Welsh, SOUTH AFRICA'S OPTIONS: STRATEGIES FOR SHARING POWER, New York, St. Martin's Press, 1979, 196pp.

Wilson, Francis, LABOR IN THE SOUTH AFRICAN GOLD MINES 1911-1969, Cambridge University Press, 1972, 218pp.

The Bantustans are the ten underdeveloped areas, most of them sited around the periphery of South Africa, that its government sees as its "answer" to the overwhelming majority of Africans in that country as compared to the rest of its inhabitants, and especially the whites. Four of the homelands--Transkei, Bophuthatswana, Venda, and Ciskei--have accepted the "independence" that only South Africa itself recognizes. Until recently it maintained that not only those of the particular ethnic identity domiciled in that territory but also all of the same ethnic lineage within South Africa itself had lost their South African citizenship. South Africa now maintains that fifty-four percent of all Africans are in the "homelands" or Bantustans and only forty-six percent in the rest of South Africa.

Since, however, South Africa's factories, mines, and offices depend so largely on African labor, there is a steady stream of migrant labor from the Bantustans. Those close enough to urban areas may travel by fast trains to and from them daily. Most of the migrants, however, are away for much longer from their families who must depend on what they earn for virtually all their livelihood.

THE BANTUSTANS

Butler, Jeffrey, Robert Rotberg, and John Adams, THE
BLACK HOMELANDS OF SOUTH AFRICA: THE POLITICAL
AND ECONOMIC DEVELOPMENT OF BOPHUTHATSWANA AND
KWA-ZULU, Berkeley, University of California Press,
1977, 250pp.

Carter, Gwendolen M., Thomas Karis, and Newell M.
Stultz, SOUTH AFRICA'S TRANSKEI, THE POLITICS OF
DOMESTIC COLONIALISM, Evanston, Northwestern Univer-
sity Press, 1967, 200pp.

Moerdijk, Donald, ANTI-DEVELOPMENT: SOUTH AFRICA AND
ITS BANTUSTANS, Paris, UNESCO Press, 1981, 194pp.

Rogers, Barbara, DIVIDE AND RULE: SOUTH AFRICAN
BANTUSTANS, London, International Defence and Aid
Fund, 1976, 86pp.

Southall, Roger J., SOUTH AFRICA'S TRANSKEI: THE
POLITICAL ECONOMY OF AN "INDEPENDENT" BANTUSTAN,
New York, Monthly Review Press, 1983, 338pp.

Namibia is in a unique situation. Controlled by
Germany up to World War I, it was invaded by the South
Africans as part of the war effort. At the war's end,
South Africa planned to turn Namibia into its fifth
province. It was prevented from this action, however,
by President Wilson's opposition to annexations at
the end of the fighting, and accepted the concept devised
by its own General Jan Smuts. As mandatory, however,
South Africa was allowed to administer and legislate
for Namibia as if it was an integral part of its own
territory.

After World War II had ended, South Africa was the
only mandatory power that refused to place its territory
under the more rigorous trusteeship system, or to grant
it independence. Moreover, it increasingly extended
its own discriminatory legislation to Namibia, including
the pass laws and the contract labor system. Finally,
a case was brought before the World Court seeking to

abrogate the mandate but it failed on the ground that Ethiopia and Liberia had no status to bring the action. This decision outraged the General Assembly of the United Nations which voted to revoke South Africa's mandate on the ground of maladministration, with the United States voting in the affirmative. By Resolution 2145, the United Nations declared South Africa's presence in the territory to be an illegal occupation, a position confirmed in an advisory opinion by the International Court of Justice. South Africa has refused to yield, however, and still remains in effective control of Namibia.

NAMIBIA

Department of Information and Publicity, SWAPO of Namibia, TO BE BORN A NATION: THE LIBERATION STRUGGLE FOR NAMIBIA, London, Zed Press, 1981, 357pp.

Gordon, Robert J., MINES, MASTERS AND MIGRANTS: LIFE IN A NAMIBIAN COMPOUND, Johannesburg, Raven Press, 279pp.

Green, Reginald H., Kimmo Kiljunen, Marja-Liisa Kiljunen, eds., NAMIBIA: THE LAST COLONY, New York, New York, 1977, Longman, 1981, 310pp.

Kerina, Mburumba, NAMIBIA: THE MAKING OF A NATION, New York, Books in Focus, Inc., 1981, 314pp.

Rocha, Geisa, Maria, IN SEARCH OF NAMIBIAN INDEPENDENCE: THE LIMITATIONS OF THE UNITED NATIONS, Boulder, Westview Press, 1984, 167pp.

Rotberg, Robert, ed., NAMIBIA: POLITICAL AND ECONOMIC PROSPECTS, Lexington, Mass., Lexington Books, D.C. Heath & Co., 1983, 133pp.

RHODESIA/ZIMBABWE

Compared to South Africa, the works available on Rhodesia and Zimbabwe, as it was renamed in 1980 when it achieved independence under African control, are relatively few. A superb, eminently readable, but

very lengthy history has been written by Professor
Arthur Keppel-Jones under the title of RHODES AND
RHODESIA: THE WHITE CONQUEST OF ZIMBABWE, 1884-1902
(McGill-Queens University Press, Kingston and Montreal,
1983, xiv, 674pp). A personal account of the struggle
for independence written by Judith Todd, daughter of
the former Rhodesian Prime Minister, Garfield Todd,
both of whom were imprisoned under the Ian Smith regime,
is THE RIGHT TO SAY NO (The Third Press, N.Y. 1973,
204pp). A much more comprehensive account of THE
STRUGGLE FOR ZIMBABWE: THE CHIMURENGA WAR, by David
Martin and Phyllis Johnson (Faber and Faber, London,
1981, 378pp) is almost an eye witness account seen
from what became the winning side. A brilliantly
prepared work by an American journalist, Julie Frederiks,
entitled NONE BUT OURSELVES: MASSES VS. MEDIA IN THE
MAKING OF ZIMBABWE (Raven Press and Zimbabwe Publishing
House, 1982, viii, 368pp) contrasts directly the
propaganda by the Ian Smith regime with the songs and
comments from the other side of the struggle which
was ultimately successful. Patrick O'Meara's
comprehensive chapter entitled "Zimbabwe: The Politics
of Independence" is in SOUTHERN AFRICA: THE CONTINUING
CRISIS, edited by Gwendolen M. Carter and Patrick O'Meara
(Indiana University Press, 1982, second edition, xii,
404pp). There is also a paperback biography of MUGABE
by David Smith & Colin Simpson published by Sphere
Books, London, 1981, 218pp.

The governments of Angola and of Mozambique, which
were former Portuguese colonies, have Marxist-Leninist
leanings. Angola has long housed Cuban troops which
support its internal struggle for power with its ethnic
rival UNITA, and against the efforts of the South African
army to overthrow its MPLA government. South Africa

uses the Cuban troops as its justification for not bringing Namibia to independence, and the Reagan administration tends to agree and also refuses to recognize the MPLA government as all other major states have done. As far as Mozambique is concerned, however, the South African government, aided by the United States, achieved what was believed to be a notable success through the N'komati Agreement signed in March 1984, through which both governments agreed to end support for the movements aided by the other: the African National Congress (ANC), the 70 year old standard bearer of African nationalism in South Africa though long exiled from that country, and the Mozambique Resistance Movement (MRM also known as RENAMO), based in and supported by South Africa after Zimbabwean independence and dangerously harrassing Mozambique. Mozambique's government acted swiftly to curb the ANC, but South Africa has not yet prevented MRM guerrillas from continuing to cause great damage in southern Mozambique, and even appears to have provided them with some support.

ANGOLA AND MOZAMBIQUE

Bender, Gerald J., ANGOLA UNDER THE PORTUGUESE: THE MYTH AND THE REALITY, Berkeley, University of California Press, 1978, 287pp.

Davidson, Basil, IN THE EYE OF THE STORM: ANGOLA'S PEOPLE, Garden City, New York, Anchor Books, Anchor Press/Doubleday, 1973, 386pp.

Hanlon, Joseph, MOZAMBIQUE: THE REVOLUTION UNDER FIRE, London, Zed Books, XIII, 1984, 292pp.

Henderson, Lawrence, (Gwendolen M. Carter, ed.), ANGOLA, FIVE CENTURIES OF CONFLICT, Ithaca, New York, Cornell University Press, 1979, 272pp.

Henricksen, Thomas H., REVOLUTION AND COUNTERREVOLUTION: MOZAMBIQUE'S WAR OF INDEPENDENCE 1964-1974, Westport, Conn., Greenwood Press, 1983, 289pp.

Isaacman, Allen and Barbara, MOZAMBIQUE: FROM COLONIALISM TO REVOLUTION 1900-1982, Boulder, Colorado, Westview Press, 1983, 235pp.

Marcum, John, THE ANGOLAN REVOLUTION, Vol. 1, Cambridge, Mass., M.I.T. Press, 1969, 380pp.; Vol. 2, Cambridge, Mass., M.I.T. Press, 1978, 473pp.

Mondlane, Eduardo, THE STRUGGLE FOR MOZAMBIQUE, London, Zed Press, 1983, 225pp.

Munslow, Barry, MOZAMBIQUE: THE REVOLUTION AND ITS ORIGINS, New York, Longman, 1983, 195pp.

Wolfers, Michael and Jane Bergerol, ANGOLA IN THE FRONTLINE, London, Zed Press, 1983, 238pp.

The Mozambique Information Agency, P.O. Box 896, Maputo, issues a useful information bulletin monthly: annual subscription $25 for institutions; $15 for individuals (includes airmail).

The Southern African Development Coordination Conference (SADCC), as already noted, has the avowed objective of reducing the dependence on South Africa of the independent African controlled states through improving their network of railways to take more advantage of their own ocean ports, and developing their potential resources in agriculture, mining and even manufacturing.

Aided by international organizations and foreign governments, SADCC has made considerable progress toward meeting its short and long term objectives. Basic questions remain, however, regarding what policies the South African government will pursue both externally within the Southern African area and internally, for the Southern African area will never experience genuine peace until its dominant power establishes more harmonious race relations within its own borders.

SADCC

Maasdorp, Gavin, SADCC: A POST-NKOMATI EVALUATION Johannesburg, The South African Institute of International Affairs, Special Study, August 1984.

Meyns, Peter, "The Southern African Development Coordi-
    nation Conference (SADCC) and Regional Cooperation
    in Southern Africa," in Domenico Mazzeo, (ed.),
    AFRICAN REGIONAL ORGANIZATIONS New York, Cambridge
    University Press, 1984, pp. 196-224.

Nsekela, Amon, (ed.), SOUTHERN AFRICA: TOWARD ECONOMIC
    LIBERATION, London, Rex Collings, 1981, 274pp.

SADCC - Maseru, The Proceedings of the Southern African
    Development Coordination Conference held in Maseru,
    Kingdom of Lesotho on January 27 & 28, 1983, Gweru,
    Zimbabwe: Mambo Press, 1983, 332pp.

Among the Southern African states that belong
to SADCC, Zambia is particularly important because
of its mineral resources, Botswana because of the leading
role it has assumed in that association, Swaziland
because of its strategic position abutting on Mozambique,
and Malawi as a link through the lake to the north.
Lesotho is land locked and completely surrounded by
South African territory and under pressure to sign
a N'komati type agreement which it has been resisting.
(Botswana, Lesotho and Swaziland are part of a customs
union with South Africa.) Tanzania, though a member
of SADCC and of the Front Line States, which worked
to secure Zimbabwean independence, does not, strictly
speaking, belong to Southern Africa because of its
geographical position.

BOTSWANA, LESOTHO, AND SWAZILAND

Booth, Alan R., SWAZILAND, TRADITION AND CHANGE IN
    A SOUTHERN AFRICAN KINGDOM, Boulder, Colorado,
    Westview Press, 1984, 145pp.

Kuper, Hilda, SOBHUZA II, NGWENYAMA AND KING OF
    SWAZILAND, New York, Africana Publishing Co., 1978,
    363pp.

Parson, Jack, BOTSWANA, LIBERAL DEMOCRACY AND THE LABOR
    RESERVE IN SOUTHERN AFRICA, Boulder, CO., Westview
    Press, 1984, 145pp.

Potholm, Christian P., SWAZILAND, THE DYNAMICS OF
    POLITICAL MODERNIZATION, Berkeley, CA., University
    of California Press, 1972, 156pp.

Stevens, Richard P., LESOTHO, BOTSWANA, AND SWAZILAND,
    THE FORMER ` HIGH COMMISSION TERRITORIES IN SOUTHERN
    AFRICA, London, Frederick A. Praeger, 1967, 266pp.

MALAWI

McMaster, Carolyn, MALAWI: FOREIGN POLICY AND DEVELOP-
    MENT, London, Julian Friedmann Publishers Ltd.,
    1974, 176pp.

Williams, T. David, (Gwendolen M. Carter, ed.) MALAWI:
    THE POLITICS OF DESPAIR, Ithaca, New York, Cornell
    University Press, 1978, 334pp.

See also the analysis of personal rule by President
    H. Kamuzu Banda, in Jackson, Robert H. and Carl
    G. Rosberg, PERSONAL RULE IN BLACK AFRICA: PRINCE,
    AUTOCRAT, PROPHET, TYRANT, Berkeley, University
    of California Press, 1982, pp. 159-167.

ZAMBIA

Kaunda, Kenneth, ZAMBIA SHALL BE FREE: AN AUTOBIOGRAPHY,
    New York, Praeger, 1963; London, Heinemann, 1962,
    202pp.

Pettman, Jan, ZAMBIA: SECURITY AND CONFLICT, Sussex,
    England, Julian Friedmann Publishers Ltd., 1974,
    241pp.

Rotberg, Robert I., BLACK HEART: GORE-BROWNE AND THE
    POLITICS OF MULTIRACIAL ZAMBIA, Berkeley, University
    of California Press, 1977, 335pp.

Sklar, Richard L., CORPORATE POWER IN AN AFRICAN STATE:
    THE POLITICAL IMPACT OF MULTINATIONAL MINING COMPANIES
    IN ZAMBIA, Berkeley, University of California Press,
    1975, 216pp.

Tordoff, William, POLITICS IN ZAMBIA, Berkeley,
    University of California Press, 1974, 401pp.

United States policies toward Southern Africa have
focused largely on its relations with South Africa,

and the latter's refusal to bring Namibia to independence. As Southern African states like Angola, Mozambique, and particularly Zimbabwe were moving toward independence, however, American policies were particularly important either in aiding, as with Rhodesia-Zimbabwe, or hampering as with Angola, the smoothness of the process. There has been a noticeable difference, also, between the attitudes of different American regimes. President Jimmy Carter was particularly supportive of the new African states, and the United Nations role in Namibia, and outspoken in criticism of South African apartheid to a much greater degree than had been those who preceeded him, and the current Ronald Reagan period of office.

Nonetheless, the issue of American investment in South Africa and the role American business should play in that country, are becoming matters of public concern. Thus the closeness of American-South African relations under the "constructive engagement" policies followed by Assistant Secretary for Africa Chester Crocker is becoming increasingly controversial.

US POLICY TOWARD SOUTH AFRICA

Clough, Michael, (ed.), CHANGING REALITIES IN SOUTHERN AFRICA: IMPLICATIONS FOR AMERICAN POLICY, Berkeley, Institute of International Studies, 1982, 318pp.

Lake, Anthony, CAUTION AND CONCERN: THE MAKING OF AMERICAN POLICY TOWARD SOUTH AFRICA, 1946-1971, University Microfilms International, Ann Arbor, Michigan, 1974, 498pp.

LeMarchand, Rene, (ed.), AMERICAN POLICY IN SOUTHERN AFRICA: THE STAKES AND THE STANCE, Washington, University Press of America, 1978, 450pp.

Ogene, F. Chidozie, INTEREST GROUPS AND THE SHAPING OF FOREIGN POLICY: FOUR CASE STUDIES OF UNITED STATES AFRICAN POLICY, St. Martin's Press, New York, 1983, 224pp.

Oye, Kenneth A., Leiber, Robert J., and Rothchild, Donald, (eds.), EAGLE DEFIANT: UNITED STATES FOREIGN POLICY IN THE 1980s, Little, Brown and Company, Boston, 1983, 404pp.

Seidman, Ann & Neva, SOUTH AFRICA AND U.S. MULTINATIONAL CORPORATIONS, Westport, Conn., Lawrence Hill & Co., 1978, 251pp.

Stockwell, John, IN SEARCH OF ENEMIES: A CIA STORY, New York, W.W. Norton, 1978, 254pp.

Western Massachusetts Association of Concerned African Scholars, (eds.), U.S. MILITARY INVOLVEMENT IN SOUTHERN AFRICA, Boston, South End Press, 1978, 276pp.

CHAPTER SIX
AFRICAN INDEPENDENCE
A RETROSPECTIVE VIEW

Independence is a heady concept and an absorbing goal.
Less surprising than that Sub-Saharan Africa, the last
great area of colonial control, was gripped by that
concept and that aim in the nineteen fifties and sixties
is that it happened so late. In the decade before,
the Asian sub-continent was rocked by and, unhappily,
torn apart by insistence on national independence during
and following World War II when the British Empire
and its European allies faced their greatest danger.
During its course, Asian and African soldiers were
drawn into combat far from their own homes. Their
new experiences, ideas, and the impact of the war itself
inevitably stimulated new aspirations for their homelands. The pledge of ultimate self-government for
all people implicit in the Atlantic Charter signed
by Prime Minister Winston Churchill and President
Franklin Roosevelt in 1941 provided nationalists throughout the world with the phrases they were to flaunt
in the years thereafter to justify their struggle against
overlordship by outside powers.

A dozen trips to Africa starting in 1948 and extending through 1972 gave me opportunities to learn at first hand something of the forces at work in the countries seeking and gaining independence during that period, and to discuss them with a wide and varied range of persons intimately involved in them. My basic research then, as now, was on South Africa, long independent in a technical sense but subject with increasing intensity to demands by its own black majority to share social and political rights. But no one, least of all I, could ignore those areas where African independence was being sought with increasing fervor and success.

I had stopped in Kenya in 1948 on my way to South Africa and been shocked at the insolence of whites toward Africans, and Indians, impressions that made me more tolerant, in fact, of what I found in South Africa. In 1953, I experienced independence fever in the Gold Coast, the sharpest possible contrast to more than a year of research on South African politics including the United Party's last effort during the 1953 election to stave off the threat of Afrikaner Nationalist control, and failing to do so.

It was chance that the first two countries of colonial Africa that I visited were Kenya and the Gold Coast but they represented two types of the African countries seeking independence. The Gold Coast (renamed Ghana after independence) was typical of those Sub-Saharan colonies with almost no white resident population. Kenya, in contrast, had a well established politically and socially dominant white resident population. Not surprisingly, there were significant differences in their evolution toward independence. Although the interval between Ghana's independence in 1957 and that of Kenya in 1963 was not long, the issue of the White Highlands had threatened its progress to independence, and also helps to explain why Southern Rhodesia only became independent Zimbabwe in 1980.

Ghanaian friends of mine used to say, "The mosquito has saved West Africa from white settler domination!" Indeed, in the days before the little white pills with which one can insulate oneself against malaria, and the shots that prevented yellow fever, long also a menace of tropical Africa though no longer so, Europeans, as they were generally called, were in great danger of contracting one or the other of these dread diseases. Where there was adequate anchorage, as off Southern Nigeria, traders could sleep on their ships and go ashore only long enough to do their business and then retreat out of range of the insects carrying the germs. As far as the Gold Coast was concerned there was no such possibility until the harbor at Tema was built near Accra. The waves come in with great power and velocity and the only way in to the mainland used to be in small boats tossing over the waves. Naturally, I preferred to fly when I arrived from South Africa in 1953.

"To go from the Union of South Africa to the Gold Coast," I wrote on my return to the United States, "is to experience an extraordinary antithesis, politically and psychologically." In South Africa, the aim of the now entrenched Afrikaner Nationalists was to exclude the African "still more completely from European society despite the completeness of his economic intermeshing." And I added: "there is almost nothing...which contributes to the self-respect of the African...." "Frustration and bitterness, growing rapidly and possibly dangerously, are the not unnatural results."

"In the Gold Coast, in contrast, transfer of political power to the Africans is already far advanced," I noted. "Despite a lingering sense of suspicion in some quarters of British intentions, which is based on the past rather than on present policies, the Gold Coast is substantially and increasingly on its own."

What I failed to realize as fully as I should have done was that the tensions between Kwame Nkrumah and the conservative elements in the country still ran deep. They were to continue to handicap the operations of government after independence had been achieved.

It was the conservatives who had brought Nkrumah back to the Gold Coast in 1947, after completing his studies in the United States, so as to organize the youth for their United Gold Coast Convention. But Nkrumah wanted an organization of his own. In 1949, he formed the Convention Peoples Party, the CPP, which reflected his own strong nationalist approach. The year before, an Ex-Servicemen's march had precipitated riots in Accra fueled by economic demands. It was those riots that led the British to begin the process that led to independence.

Nkrumah called the proposed constitution "bogus and fraudulent" and was in jail because of his protests when the 1951 election was held in which his party gained a decisive majority. He was instantly released, and within hours was brought with his top associates to Christiansborg Castle where the Governor, Sir Charles Arden-Clarke, told them that they were the responsible ministers of the new government. In the ensuing period until independence, the Governor unobtrusively helped to prepare them to handle the manifold tasks and problems of government.

The first African country to emerge from colonial control (which neither Liberia nor Ethiopia experienced), the Gold Coast had advantages few other African states could match: the gold that gave it its name; rich manganese resources; above all, the cocoa bean. Its cultivation by peasant proprietors, and the local handling of its distribution and sale provided the Gold Coast with both a well established largely landed African proletariat and a burgeoning middle class, the most substantial one in colonial Africa. Its contacts with European traders--Dutch, Danes, Swedes, Portuguese, and British--were said locally to stretch all the way back to Christopher Columbus on a trip before he reached America.

But there were also ferments within the country that would complicate the path to independence and thereafter. I perceived three revolutions going on at the same time in 1953. There was youth against age and traditional authority which was represented by the chiefs and supported by members of the opposition; another pitted the proletariat against the bourgeoisie; and the third, the least worrisome, was that of the people of the Gold Coast against the British government, and its control.

In fact, the transfer of power was taking place smoothly once the new government learned that it had to provide the resources to implement its sometimes grandiose plans. When I asked Nkrumah in 1953 what were the greatest difficulties they faced in the transfer of power, he said immediately: "Developing the civil service, and maintaining the constitutional advance." It seemed to me, however, that he did not realize the difficulties in training administrative personnel, and overestimated the ease with which Africanization could be achieved satisfactorily. At the same time, he seemed to anticipate that technical personnel would continue to be European for a considerable time to come.

In 1953, I already saw significant shifts in the prestige and power of two groups: the traditional authority of the chiefs, and from the bourgeoisie to the proletariat. I visited one of the more conservative of the chiefs, Nana Afori Atta II, on the day of the traditional ceremony of bringing the golden stool and linguistic stick from their sanctuary and watched the people dance to the beat of the drums. Nana and the district commissioner both spoke regretfully of the

rapidity of the change going on. Although a close
relative of Dr. Danquet, the leader of the opposition,
Nana was wise enough to bow to the inevitable. Without
the British to support their authority, the chiefs
would progressively lose their power. Some who stood
out against the wishes of the young had already been
destooled. Others, like La Mantse of Labadi, a suburb
of Accra, had moved full circle from being an open
opponent of Nkrumah to becoming, at least overtly,
a strong nationalist.

The CPP was "a radical, somewhat left wing party,"
in my view with a "group of trained intellectuals as
its ministers." I foresaw potential problems from
the pressures of its left wing trade unionists, which
had official links with the WFTU in Vienna. The position
of the opposition that called itself the United Party,
worried me more. It was pushing the CPP to work harder
for independence on the misguided expectation that
it would win the next election itself. It believed
its own leaders were "more experienced and more sober"
than those of the CPP but, to me, it lacked "a constructive, alternative program."

Among the opposition's supporters were the highly
conservative Mohammedans, most of whom lived in the
largely undeveloped Northern Territories, due to have
its first election shortly, and subsequently a troubled
spot. The Mohammedans were openly antagonistic toward
Nkrumah over his refusal to increase their representation
on the Accra Town Council. It seemed just one more
sign of the lack of a common allegiance to the country's
government and its leader. Another weakness seemed
the heavy dependence for foreign exchange on cocoa,
a monoculture. Yet, on balance, I felt that of all
the areas of colonial Africa, the Gold Coast had the
best chance of making its independence work.

When I returned to independent Ghana in October
1958, I found that my earlier fears regarding relations
between the government and the opposition were more

than justified. After pleasantries, and congratulations on the very noticeable advances in road building, establishing a new port, and accelerating the growth of the university (though secondary education seemed stagnant), I touched on the most sensitive issue. "I believe that in a democratic system, the opposition is a key factor because it keeps the government responsible for publicly justifying its acts," I said, as I sat opposite Prime Minister Kwame Nkrumah in the same room in Christiansborg Castle where before I had talked with the Governor. "Yet outside Ghana and inside it too, I hear constantly that it is difficult even for the official opposition to express criticisms of your party and your administration for fear of reprisals." He frowned quickly and then said "I feel the same way that you do about the opposition.... But when I ask the opposition to sit around the table with me and give me their criticisms, they will not do so. They organize in cells and they plan violence. What can I do if they threaten to assassinate me?"

"Impatient of forms which appeared to impede his program, irritated by advice to select priorities rather than move forward on all fronts at once," I wrote when I returned to the hotel, "Nkrumah, with his vivid, oversensitized imagination was seized above all with the fear of violence and of the danger that death might end his plans for his nation." That there had been an assassination plot seemed clear but it had been unbelievably badly planned. In retaliation, there had been arbitrary deportations, and restraints on the opposition's meetings at election time.

Excesses by both sides had had serious consequences. In 1954, there had been anti-government violence in Kumasi, the historic center of Ashanti, which was both the wealthiest part of the country and the chief center of resistance to the CPP. Order was eventually established but rather harshly. The opposition United Party protested the government's action by unwisely boycotting the 1958 elections for the Regional Assemblies. This opened the way for the CPP to gain control of all five Regional Assemblies, and then to vote them out of existence.

Thus the restraint on central power, which the British had insisted should be inserted in the constitution, was eliminated without a struggle. Nkrumah's own comment to me when I saw him on October 30, 1958, was "The opposition insisted on the Regional Assemblies, and the British government made us accept them if we were to have independence. Now we can dispose of that and get a government that really works."

Although Nkrumah endorsed a role for the chiefs, it was as agents of the government with no separate basis of power such as they had possessed traditionally. As a capstone to centralization of power, Ghana became a republic in 1960 and Nkrumah its president not through any special testing of popular approval but by virtue of the votes of his parliamentary majority.

It was the equating of democracy with a universal franchise and no restraints on the actions of the party in power. Unfortunately, this was, and has remained all too common throughout Africa. It contrasts sharply with our belief that while democracy involves the rule of the majority, that rule should be exercised with accepted restraints, whether written ones as in this country, or implicit as in Great Britain.

The British had at least provided some built-in restraints, notably the Regional Assemblies so soon discarded, and a considerable amount of training before the Gold Coast was launched on independence. The next in line, Guinea, had neither when it took independence in 1958. What President Charles deGaulle had offered it, as to all the French African territories, in his famous speech at Brazzaville in August, 1958, was membership in the Franco-African Community which, unlike

the British Commonwealth, had common organs, notably
its Executive Committee on which the premiers of the
twelve French African territories and of France were
to sit along with the relevant French ministers.

When deGaulle visited Conakry immediately afterwards,
Sekou Toure made a deliberately provocative speech
declaring that "If we can have independence and association with France, we wish it. But if we must choose
between being rich through an association with France,
which prevents independence, and being poor and independent, we prefer independence." DeGaulle, affronted,
answered in kind. When the vote on membership in the
Franco-African Community was held, Guinea voted "Non."

Immediately, as was clearly apparent during my visit
there in mid-November 1958, almost all the 4,000 French
administrators, technicians, doctors, judges and
soldiers, presented abruptly with the choice between
returning at once to France or remaining permanently
as part of Guinea's administration, had left or were
leaving, many of them regretfully. The only posts
to which they were allowed to return without forfeiting
their French connection were in the schools. As I
wrote at the time, "The concentrated amount of
inexperience which is trying to cope with the business
of government and social services is overwhelming."
It does appear, however, that some senior personnel,
with the Commissioner of Ports and of the Railways
among them, offered to stay and were refused. So it
cut both ways.

Guinea had not long to wait for outside support.
Ghana recognized its independence within forty-eight
hours, and provided some financial aid. There was
a brief but inaccurate report of a Ghana-Guinea Union,
which temporarily alarmed the British at the prospect
of a French-speaking member other than Quebec in the
Commonwealth! Senegal lent much needed personnel,
Czechoslovakia sent arms and medical supplies, the

Chinese and Americans sent food. Six Communist countries signed trade agreements with Guinea, raising apprehensions of an Eastern alignment. But as a local Communist sympathizer said to me in Conakry: "We cannot have Communism in this country. There is no class struggle to begin with....And, obviously, we are in the Western area of the world even if we wanted it otherwise."

The Ivory Coast, lying between Guinea and Ghana, had its own problems in October 1958 when well-planned internal riots drove eight to ten thousand Dahomean, Togolese and Yoruba refugees into the Old Port, victims of their own effective roles in administration and business. Even President Houphouet-Boigny, when he returned from Paris, could not repair the damage. Most of the outcasts had to be repatriated to their homes to the detriment of the Ivory Coast itself. After fifteen years of spending much of his time in Paris, even Houphouet-Boigny was forced to recognize that the locus of power was now in his own capital. He moved rapidly to secure full independence and United Nations membership in July 1960. But he also retained his close links with France for good economic reasons: the protected position of the Ivory Coast within the French market and thus ultimately within the European Common Market for products like coffee, which represented one half of the value of the Ivory Coast's exports.

On the opposite side of the African continent, much had been going on in Kenya and Tanganyika. The former had been racked by the MauMau terrorism that reflected bitterness at the entrenched position of the white settlers, and their exclusive rights to the so-called White Highlands. When I took my Smith College students there in the summer of 1957, the atmosphere was still tense and divisions apparent.

I well remember that after we listened to a debate in the Assembly, Tom Mboya, one of the most dynamic

of the younger nationalists, said bitterly to me:
"Why didn't you let me know you were coming and we
would have said much more about our grievances." When
I invited him to the hotel and we sat together on the
verandah outside my room which faced into the courtyard,
African servants kept passing to and fro looking up
in amazement that Mboya was allowed to be there. I
understood, because in 1952 Mboya could not even enter
the hotel (nor, incidently, were its Indian owners)
and he and I had to discuss plans for our new Kikuyu
Smith College student, Florence Mwangi, while standing
in the dusk outside so as not to attract attention.

When I returned in 1959, there were striking changes,
although the state of emergency was still officially
in existence. The program of bringing peasants from
the Kiambu area south of Nairobi, Nyeri, and Fort Hall
where MauMau activity had been most severe was being
reversed. Villagization was not only essential for
the protection of the Kikuku themselves and their control
by the security forces but also made health measures
and experience with sanitation possible, and even some
schooling though teachers were scarce. During my visit,
I could see the process of moving those with three
or more acres back to their farms. Everywhere houses
were going up; 10,000 would be needed. Those peasants
with less than three acres or no land at all were if
possible, I was told, to be assigned an eighth of an
acre in a newly built village.

Decisive in underpinning this migration back to
the farms had been land consolidation. Kikuyu land
holdings had been subdivided over and over again among
wives and for sons with endless litigation going on
in the process. The farms to which the peasants were
returning were consolidated areas running from the
top of ridges to the bottom in accordance with custom,
and divided by fences. Coffee, tea, and, less often,
pyrethium, the base for DDT, were on the slopes, and

maize below. The British aim: a landed peasantry as a "brake on agitation," said a District Officer, but not all had land to return to.

Kenya's political tensions needed a constitutional outlet. There were several answers being offered to meet this need. Michael Blundell's multi-racial New Kenya Group, supported by about half the European settlers and the British Colonial Office, proposed a common roll but with school leaving certificates as qualifications, high under existing circumstances. He told me privately that he foresaw a span of seventeen to twenty-seven years before independence. Tom Mboya and the African elected members of the Legislative Council wanted universal franchise in 1960; no guaranteed rights for Europeans including those in the White Highlands or for Asians; but about one-third of the seats reserved in the Legislative Assembly for minority or special groups like Mboya's own trade unionists; a Council of Ministers presumably drawn from the African majority; a short period of responsible government under British supervision; and then independence. He favored Nigeria's example of a federal state with only limited, though growing powers vested in the central government, and was concerned at Nkrumah's arbitrary actions in Ghana toward the opposition.

Spurring Mboya's timetable for independence was the rapid advance toward independence in Tanganyika, a British Trust Territory, whose outstanding political figure then, as now, was Julius Nyerere. By great good fortune, Nyerere happened to be in Nairobi in late June, 1959, when we were there and spoke with great pride of his all-African party, TANU, the Tanganyika African National Union, and of his own European deputy, Derek Bryceson, in TEMO, the multi-racial Tanganyika Elected Members Organization. TANU had only begun in 1954 but grew so rapidly that neither the British nor the chiefs were aware of its strength until the first election in September 1958 for half the country's constituencies. In a novel form of franchise, each voter had to vote for a European, an Asian, and an African.

In the second election held in February, 1959, for the rest of the constituencies, TANU's victory was even more decisive. When we were in Dar-es-Salaam, we were entertained by five new ministers, the first to be drawn from the elected members. It says much for the bonds Nyerere had welded that two of them, Bryceson (incidently the second husband of Jane Goodall who still produces magnificent wild life films), and Amir Jamal, treasurer of TEMU, remained his close political associates throughout their lifetimes.

Although Tom Mboya was disappointed that Tanganyika received its independence two years earlier than Kenya did, it is remarkable that the latter also earned that status as early as 1963. Jomo Kenyatta, when released from protective custody in the Northern Province, proved to be much more than "the spent force" that was Mboya's expectation in 1959, and his stature and moderation were major factors in the speed with which events moved thereafter. It also helped that Malcolm MacDonald, son of the former British Prime Minister, Ramsay MacDonald, and Kenyatta worked together in much the same way as Alden-Clark and Nkrumah had done to prepare the Gold Coast for independence in 1957.

There was one special incident at which I was present which made me realize how much Kenyatta did personally to overbridge divisions in his country before independence. In August, 1963, when I was in Kenya briefly, I learned that Kenyatta was going to Nakuru, in the heart of the White Highlands, to meet with many of the European settlers who formed the core of opposition to the ending of British rule. My companion from the American Consulate and I reached the large shed early but its rows of seats were already full with rather grim looking men and women, many of whom looked weather beaten from working in their fields along side their staffs. We stood at the back to watch.

Presently, there was the sound of a car, then shuffling of feet and Kenyatta entered near where we were standing. He paused, straightened himself, and began to move slowly up toward the platform. He passed several rows before there was any movement. Then one or two stood up, those behind them did likewise, and soon the whole audience was standing and applauding. Kenyatta relaxed, went nimbly up the steps to the platform, turned and faced them, and began, "Fellow farmers! You know they steal my cows too." The room rocked with laughter, and he was on his way over his greatest hurdle. He pledged his support to all who farmed their land productively, a pledge repeated in his first speech after independence. Many white settlers were to remain to do so. I am not the only one who wonders whether Kenyatta might have forestalled or limited MauMau terror had he not been kept imprisoned so long by the British.

Kenyan independence was the one such celebration to which I was invited and it remains a glowing memory. For the one and only time in my life, I flew first class to England and on to Kenya (at my own expense I hasten to say). Moreover, I ousted a Cabinet minister from the front row on the latter lap! During the week-long festivities, I found myself torn between watching gay dances and other extravaganzas (many of which I still have on movie film, I hope), and talking with the many other people who had been invited, some of whom had only been deeply respected names up to that time. I remember, in particular, Chairman Lall, who was sent by Nehru to conduct Kenyatta's defense and as an Asian was not allowed into Nyeri at night and had to sleep on the verandah of an African grocer; Judge Thurgood Marshall with whom I shared a car; Barbara

Castle and Elwyn Jones, both M.P.'s from England; Ralph Bunche, an old friend; and many others.

The day before the main ceremony, a group of us attended the rehearsal of the great panorama of dances that had been planned. Somewhat incongruously, Mboya had insisted that the otherwise bare breasted girls should wear strips of cloth across their bosoms! Great bleachers had been erected and soldiers sent to run up and down them as forcefully as they could to be sure they would not collapse at some vital moment. A special parking lot had been prepared on the other side of the road but an inquisitive lion from the nearby game reserve had wandered in and had to be shooed out. It was a great day!

Then came the ceremony itself, held at night as independence was to come at the stroke of midnight. The stands were full to overflowing. I found myself squeezed between two large gentlemen, an African and an Asian, for whom the heat was even more trying than for me. "It's harambe," the Kenyatta slogan of comradeship, they said, as I tried to breathe.

Finally, midnight approached. The crowd suddenly hushed and Kenyatta and Prince Philip walked across the field toward the standard. Kenyatta swayed perceptibly and Prince Philip took his arm for a moment. Later, the story passed around that he whispered: "It's not too late to change your mind!" But then they stood before the standard; the lights went out; as the Union Jack came slowly down, the band broke into God Save the Queen (who had, in fact, become Queen while at Treetops in Kenya six years before); and then broke into the Kenya national anthem as the lights came on and its own flag went to the top of the mast. The audience shouted its hurrahs! Kenya was an independent state.

In a decade of travel throughout much of Sub-Saharan Africa from 1953 through 1963, I had had rich experiences in countries graduating to, or seizing independence and, in a number of instances, opportunities to talk with their leaders about their aspirations.

With a former Smith College student, Amanda Fisk, I had motored 3,000 miles through much of the Belgian Congo, admiring its roads and ferries, and its vast mining establishments. But I worried that, unlike the British and the French, the Belgians were only starting to provide self-governing institutions at the local level, and not at all at the provincial and national levels, as was happening in other colonies. I was, therefore, fearful with good reason, that as independence fever burgeoned in the Congo's vast area, it would lack national leadership to direct it. In Angola, which I also visited, only the Protestant missionaries appeared to understand the need for African experience in self-government while the Portuguese, who considered it still an integral part of Portugal itself, appeared to envision it mainly as a place where their own peasants could be sent to reduce the pressures on the land at home.

From Luanda in Angola, I had flown to Douala in the Cameroons where the heat and the carryover from an earlier collapse made it necessary for me to change partners for the rest of the trip. Fortunately, there was excellent medical attention for Amanda so I had no worries about her; meanwhile in Yaounde, Sally Cutler, the wife of the American consul and another former Smith College student of mine, was waiting eagerly to say she was going to travel the rest of the way with me. Several interesting days in the Cameroons were succeeded by weeks in Nigeria where we began by staying with the British Governor, which was quite an experience. Thereafter, we travelled quite widely through its regions with both British and American help in making our contacts.

Nigeria seemed far more promising than anywhere else I had been and in certain respects has proved so. Ghana again, then Sierra Leone, again entertained by the Governor, and on to bits of former French Africa. The ties of the Franco-African Community were still holding but more tenuously.

In 1958 and 1959, in the course of two separate trips, I had again travelled widely in Southern, Central and West Africa. I returned to what was by then independent Ghana; to Guinea which was following it to independence although, as already noted, on a rockier road; and to the Ivory Coast, Senegal, the Cameroons and French Equatorial Africa, which were to feel or had already felt the reverberations of Guinea's ejection from the French-African Community because of seizing that independence. Former British colonies or Trust territories like Ghana, Nigeria, Kenya, and Tanzania, offered me a fascinating array of contrasts.

Nigeria seemed, and remained somewhat stabilized by its federal divisions reflecting the obvious ethnic differences of its major regions; Ghana, in contrast, had soon disposed of even its Regional Authorities and became, therefore, subject to the often fitful will of its ruling majority and leader. Among those states that had substantial European and Asian minorities, Tanzania, then as now led by Julius Nyerere, had established the most harmonious working relationship. Its less successful, socially motivated economic experiments were still ahead. Kenya, with the shadow of MauMau behind it, was well on the way to a different but also fairly harmonious relation between Africans and Europeans, economically as well as politically.

In each of these situations, African leadership had been a crucial factor as was also the case with the former French territories. The Ivory Coast and Senegal developed a balancing relationship between their own independence and their role in the Franco-

African Community. Guinea, the maverick, was making do but much less comfortably.

The most worrisome situations were those of the Belgian Congo and Angola. The former, achieving independence in 1960 with a minimum of experience, was racked by insecurity and conflict that drew in international rivalries and organizations that long complicated its development. Angola was still in its tight Portuguese vice. Some of these experiences and my early judgements are included in a Praeger paperback entitled Independence for Africa published in 1960. Some of my conclusions formed part of my presidential address at the African Studies Association meetings, 1959. Some are drawn from sketches, letters, and other records I am only now beginning to sort and reread.

South Africa needed and got a book of its own in 1959: The Politics of Inequality: South Africa since 1948. It is probably the best but was far from the last I have written either alone as it was or with others on that compelling but vastly disturbing country, that changes continually but basically still remains much the same.

ACKNOWLEDGEMENTS

Special thanks are due to various organizations and
individuals for the support that has allowed the chapters
in this book to be brought together in their present
format. Chapter Two, "Coercive Rule in South Africa,"
is a revised version of a paper originally presented
at the Smithsonian Institution, Washington, D.C., on
December 9, 1983, as part of its eighth international
symposium, "The Road After 1984: High Technology and
Human Freedom." It will be published in 1986 in a
volume based on the symposium edited by Dr. Lewis Lapham.
I presented the original version of Chapter Three,
"United States Policies Toward South Africa and Namibia,"
at a conference on "U.S. Policy Toward Africa," September
19-20, 1984, sponsored by The Washington Institute
for Values in Public Policy. Dr. Elliott P. Skinner,
the Franz Boas Professor of Anthropology at Columbia
University and former U.S. Ambassador to Upper Volta,
chaired the conference.

The basic material for Chapter Four, "Will SADCC
Succeed?," was secured during a research trip supported
by the Ford Foundation which enabled me and my assistant,
William Cyrus Reed, to spend three months, March through

May of 1982, consulting with specialists in the SADCC states. Subsequently, I was a participant in the conference on SADCC held by the Commonwealth Institution in London, July 18-20, 1984. Chapter Six, "African Independence: A Retrospective View," was the introductory lecture in a series held at Indiana University in the Fall of 1983 from which was developed the material for African Independence: The First Twenty-Five Years edited by Patrick O'Meara and myself and published by the Indiana University Press in 1985. This article is also to be published late in 1985 in the Africana Journal.

Special thanks are due to Indiana University Press for permission to reprint the map "Southern Africa."

I would like to express my thanks to Dr. R. Hunt Davis, Jr., Director of the Center for African Studies at the University of Florida, who conceived and has wholeheartedly supported the plan to bring together under one cover these essays and speeches, and to Professor Ronald Cohen whose imagination and energetic leadership have underpinned the public success of the Carter Lecture Series. I also would like to acknowledge with appreciation the Center for African Studies staff: Carol Lauriault for her expert editorial assistance; Codey Watson for compiling the index; and Robin Sumner who prepared the manuscript for publication.

Gwendolen M. Carter
Orange City, Florida
August 1985

LIST OF ACRONYMS

ADB	African Development Bank
ANC	African National Congress
AZAPO	Azania People's Organization
BLS	Botswana, Lesotho, and Swaziland
CIA	Central Intelligence Agency
CPP	Convention People's Party
CUSA	Council of Unions of South Africa
DPSA	Detainees' Parents' Support Committee
EEC	European Economic Community (or Common Market)
FAO	Food and Agriculture Organization
FOSATU	Federation of South African Trade Unions
FSAM	Free South African Movement
.ICRISAT	International Crops Research Institution for Semi-Arid Tropics
IMF	International Monetary Fund
MFA	Multi-Fiber Arrangement
MNR	Mozambique Resistance Movement; also known as RENAMO
MPLA	People's Movement for the Liberation of Angola
MULPOC	Multinational Programing and Operational Center
PAC	Pan Africanist Congress
PTA	Preferential Trade Agreement Area
RENAMO	Mozambique Resistance Movement, also known as MNR
SADCC	Southern Africa Development Coordination Conference
SATCC	Southern African Transport and Communications Commission
SWAPO	South West African People's Organization
TANU	Tanganyika African National Union
TEMO	Tanganyika Elected Members Organization
UAW	United Auto Workers
UDF	United Democratic Front
UDI	Unilateral Declaration of Independence (November 11, 1965, Rhodesia)
UNITA	Union for the Total Independence of Angola
USAID	United States Agency for International Development

INDEX